Everyday Mathematics®

Student Math Journal 2

**The University of Chicago
School Mathematics Project**

 **Wright Group**

The McGraw-Hill Companies

USCMP Elementary Materials Component
Max Bell, Director

Authors

Max Bell
John Bretzlauf
Amy Dillard
Robert Hartfield
Andy Isaacs

James McBride, Director
Kathleen Pitvorec
Peter Saecker
Robert Balfanz*
William Carroll*

Technical Art
Diana Barrie

*First Edition only

Photo Credits
Phil Martin/Photography

Contributors
Ann Brown, Sarah Busse, Terry DeJong, Craig Dezell, John Dini, James Flanders, Donna
Goffron, Steve Heckley, Karen Hedberg, Deborah Arron Leslie, Sharon McHugh, Janet M.
Meyers, Donna Owen, William D. Pattison, Marilyn Pavlak, Jane Picken, Denise Porter,
Kelly Porto, John Sabol, Rose Ann Simpson, Debbi Suhajda, Laura Sunseri, Jayme Tighe,
Andrea Tyrance, Kim Van Haitsma, Mary Wilson, Nancy Wilson, Jackie Winston, Carl
Zmola, Theresa Zmola

This material is based upon work supported by the National Science Foundation under
Grant No. ESI-9252984. Any opinions, findings, and conclusions or recommendations
expressed in this material are those of the authors and do not necessarily reflect the views
of the National Science Foundation.

Wright Group

Send all inquiries to:
Wright Group/McGraw-Hill
P.O. Box 812960
Chicago, IL 60681

Printed in the United States of America.

ISBN 0-07-600060-5

5 6 7 8 9 10 DBH 08 07 06 05

The McGraw-Hill Companies

Contents

Unit 6: Number Systems and Algebra Concepts

A note at the bottom of each journal page indicates when that page is first used. Some pages will be used again during the course of the year.

Unit 7: Probability and Discrete Mathematics

Unit 8: Rates and Ratios

Unit 9: More about Variables, Formulas, and Graphs

Unit 10: Geometry Topics

Multiplication and Division Properties

1. **a.** If you multiply a number by 1, what number do you get? _____

   b. Give an example for each kind of number.

   Whole number _____   Fraction _____

   Decimal _____

   c. Complete: If y is a whole number, fraction, or decimal,

   then $y * 1 =$ _____ and $1 * y =$ _____ .

2. **a.** If you divide a number by 1, what number do you get? _____

   b. Give an example for each kind of number.

   Whole number _____   Fraction _____

   Decimal _____

   c. Complete: If y is a whole number, fraction, or decimal,

   then $y / 1 =$ _____ and $\frac{y}{1} =$ _____ .

3. **a.** If you divide any number, except 0, by itself, what number do you get?

   _____

   b. Give an example for each kind of number.

   Whole number _____   Fraction _____

   Decimal _____

   c. Complete: If y is any whole number, fraction, or decimal, except 0,

   then $y / y =$ _____ and $\frac{y}{y} =$ _____ .

4. Suppose you want to explain to a third grader how to solve the problem $\frac{2}{3} * \frac{3}{5}$. What will you say? Be sure to use words the third grader already knows or define any words he or she may not know.

   _____

   _____

   _____

Fraction Multiplication

Multiply. Write your answers in simplest form. When you and your partner have finished solving the problems, compare your answers. If you disagree on an answer, check it with a calculator.

1. $\frac{5}{6} * \frac{3}{10} =$ _____

2. $6 * \frac{2}{3} =$ _____

3. $7 * \frac{3}{7} =$ _____

4. $2\frac{3}{4} * \frac{4}{1} =$ _____

5. $2\frac{3}{5} * 1\frac{2}{3} =$ _____

6. $\frac{7}{3} * \frac{1}{3} =$ _____

7. $\frac{1}{4} * \frac{2}{5} =$ _____

8. $3\frac{3}{8} * \frac{3}{4} =$ _____

9. $1\frac{5}{6} * 4\frac{2}{3} =$ _____

10. $\frac{7}{10} * 2\frac{3}{5} =$ _____

11. $\frac{5}{6} * \frac{6}{5} =$ _____

12. $\frac{3}{4} * \frac{4}{3} =$ _____

13. $\frac{4}{1} * \frac{1}{4} =$ _____

14. $\frac{1}{100} * \frac{100}{1} =$ _____

15. $\frac{7}{8} * \frac{8}{7} =$ _____

16. $\frac{11}{12} * \frac{12}{11} =$ _____

17. What pattern do you notice in Problems 11–16?

_____

_____

18. $\frac{2}{3} *$ _____ $= 1$

19. $\frac{3}{5} *$ _____ $= 1$

20. Make up three multiplication problems that have 1 as the answer.

    a. _____ * _____ $= 1$ **b.** _____ * _____ $= 1$

    c. _____ * _____ $= 1$

                                                        Use with Lesson 6.1.

Reciprocals

Reciprocal Property

If a and b are any numbers, except 0, then $\frac{a}{b} * \frac{b}{a} = 1$.

$\frac{a}{b}$ and $\frac{b}{a}$ are called reciprocals of each other.

$a * \frac{1}{a} = 1$, so a and $\frac{1}{a}$ are reciprocals of each other.

Find the reciprocal of each number. Then check your answers with a calculator.

1. 6 _____

2. 17 _____

3. $\frac{3}{4}$ _____

4. $\frac{1}{3}$ _____

5. $\frac{3}{8}$ _____

6. $\frac{13}{16}$ _____

7. $8\frac{1}{2}$ _____

8. $3\frac{5}{6}$ _____

9. $4\frac{2}{3}$ _____

10. $6\frac{1}{4}$ _____

11. 0.1 _____

12. 0.4 _____

13. 0.75 _____

14. 2.5 _____

15. 0.375 _____

16. 5.6 _____

17. π (*Hint:* Use either 3.14 or $3\frac{1}{7}$ as an approximate value for π.) _____

The year didn't always begin in January. Thousands of years ago, the Roman new year began in March. This is why our months September, October, November, and December have the prefixes they do—they used to be the seventh, eighth, ninth, and tenth months, respectively. Later, the Romans added January and February to the beginning of the year. The old names for the months September through December didn't make sense then, but the Romans kept them anyway.

Renaming Fractions

Find 3 equivalent fractions for each of the fractions below.

1. $\frac{3}{5}$ _____

2. $\frac{7}{12}$ _____

3. $\frac{16}{20}$ _____

Find the missing numbers.

4. $\frac{3}{8} = \frac{x}{24}$ $x =$ _____

5. $\frac{15}{25} = \frac{n}{5}$ $n =$ _____

6. $\frac{8}{12} = \frac{f}{36} = \frac{t}{3}$ $f =$ _____ $t =$ _____

7. $\frac{7}{10} = \frac{m}{100}$ $m =$ _____

8. $\frac{6}{9} = \frac{y}{3} = \frac{z}{6}$ $y =$ _____ $z =$ _____

9. $\frac{10}{15} = \frac{w}{6}$ $w =$ _____

10. Explain how you found w in Problem 9.

_____

_____

_____

11. Make up one of your own problems.

_____ = _____ = _____

12. Solve Problem 11 in your partner's journal.

Math Boxes 6.1

1. You draw one card at random from a regular deck of 52 playing cards (no jokers). What is the chance of drawing a(n)

   a. 4? _____

   b. card with a prime number?

   _____

   c. face card (jack, queen, or king)?

   _____

   d. even-numbered black card?

   _____

142

2. a. Use your Geometry Template to draw sectors of this spinner and color them so that the chances of landing on these colors are as follows:

   red: $\frac{3}{10}$

   blue: 0.33

   green: 20%

  b. On this spinner, what is the chance of *not* landing on red, blue, or green? _____

140

3. The distance from New York to San Francisco is about 2,930 miles. A bus made this trip in 6 days. On average, about how many miles did the bus travel each day?

_____

240 241

4. Rename each mixed number as a fraction.

   a. $3\frac{7}{8}$ = _____

   b. _____ = $5\frac{8}{9}$

   c. _____ = $8\frac{5}{6}$

   d. _____ = $6\frac{9}{7}$

   e. $14\frac{2}{3}$ = _____

66

5. Circle the number sentence that describes the numbers in the table.

x	y
3	11
5	15
0	5
10	25

   $y = x + 10$

   $(2 * x) + 5 = y$

   $y - 2 = (5 - x)$

   $y - 8 = x$

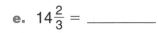
223–225

6. Write each number using digits. Then round each number to the nearest tenth.

   a. Twenty-five thousand, four hundred ten and eight hundredths

   number _____

   rounded _____

   b. Fifty-nine and six hundred seventy-two thousandths

   number _____

   rounded _____

54

Dividing Fractions and Mixed Numbers

Math Message

Solve the problems. Use a ruler to help you.

1. How many 3-centimeter segments are there in 12 centimeters? _____

2. How many $\frac{1}{2}$-inch segments are there in 4 inches? _____

3. How many $\frac{3}{4}$-inch segments are there in 3 inches? _____

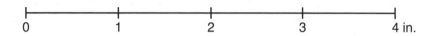

4. How many $\frac{3}{4}$-inch segments are there in $4\frac{1}{2}$ inches? _____

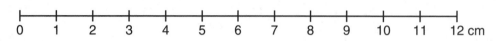

> ### Division of Fractions Algorithm
>
> $$\frac{a}{b} \div \frac{c}{d} = \frac{a}{b} * \frac{d}{c}$$

Divide. Show your work. Write your answers in simplest form.

5. $\frac{3}{8} \div \frac{5}{6} =$ _____

6. $\frac{4}{7} \div \frac{2}{3} =$ _____

7. $\frac{3}{10} \div \frac{3}{5} =$ _____

8. $\frac{11}{12} \div \frac{8}{5} =$ _____

Use with Lesson 6.2.

Dividing Fractions and Mixed Numbers (cont.)

Divide. Show your work. Write your answers in simplest form.

9. $\dfrac{7}{8} \div \dfrac{4}{9} =$ _____

10. $\dfrac{7}{12} \div \dfrac{1}{3} =$ _____

11. $\dfrac{5}{9} \div \dfrac{1}{10} =$ _____

12. $\dfrac{3}{4} \div \dfrac{7}{8} =$ _____

13. $\dfrac{5}{3} \div \dfrac{3}{5} =$ _____

14. $\dfrac{9}{10} \div \dfrac{2}{3} =$ _____

15. $1\dfrac{5}{8} \div \dfrac{4}{6} =$ _____

16. $\dfrac{3}{8} \div \dfrac{8}{2} =$ _____

17. $\dfrac{5}{4} \div \dfrac{16}{8} =$ _____

18. $1\dfrac{2}{3} \div 2\dfrac{1}{4} =$ _____

19. $\dfrac{8}{9} \div \dfrac{8}{9} =$ _____

20. $3\dfrac{7}{8} \div 1\dfrac{3}{4} =$ _____

21. Explain how you found your answer to Problem 19.

_____

_____

_____

22. Explain how you found your answer to Problem 20.

_____

_____

_____

Math Boxes 6.2

1. Write a percent for each fraction.

a. $\frac{4}{5} =$ _____

b. $\frac{8}{12} =$ _____

c. $\frac{7}{8} =$ _____

d. $\frac{3}{4} =$ _____

e. $\frac{2}{3} =$ _____

2. I am a 3-dimensional geometric shape. I have 5 faces. One face is a rectangle. The other faces are triangles.

I am called a

_____.

3. Add or subtract.

a. $3\frac{2}{3} + 1\frac{4}{5} =$ _____

b. $8\frac{1}{7} - 3\frac{3}{4} =$ _____

c. $6\frac{1}{8} - 4\frac{5}{6} =$ _____

d. $\frac{8}{5} + 3\frac{1}{9} =$ _____

4. Write the reciprocal.

a. $\frac{3}{8}$ _____

b. $\frac{5}{9}$ _____

c. $1\frac{3}{4}$ _____

d. 0.68 _____

e. 2.3 _____

5. Estimate each product by rounding the larger factor to the nearest ten-thousand.

a. $313{,}457 * 5$ _____

b. $2{,}773{,}029 * 2$ _____

c. $49{,}221 * 30$ _____

d. $12 * 402{,}655$ _____

6. Divide.

a. $8\overline{)409}$ b. $14\overline{)9{,}579}$

Use with Lesson 6.2.

Negative Numbers on a Calculator

Math Message

Read the section "Negative Numbers" on page 91 in your *Student Reference Book.*
Then use your calculator to solve the problems below. You will use the following
keys: ⬚, ⬚, ⬚, and ⬚.

1. Enter each number into your calculator. Press Enter. Record the calculator display.

   Enter   −236   −4.85 $-(\frac{2}{3})$ −0.006 $(-4)^2$ $(-8)^5$

   Display   _____   _____   _____   _____   _____   _____

The negative sign can be used to represent the phrase "the opposite of." For example,
to enter the opposite of 12, key in ⬚ 12 Enter. The display shows −12. To enter the
opposite of −12, key in ⬚ ⬚ 12 Enter. The display shows 12. We can write "the
opposite of −12" as "−(−12)" or as "(OPP) (−12)." The symbol (OPP) is read "the
opposite of."

2. Enter each number into your calculator. Record the calculator display. Clear.

   Enter   (OPP) 75   (OPP) (−89)   (OPP) (−312)   (OPP) (27 − 16)   (OPP) (−18 + 56)

   Display   _____   _____   _____   _____   _____

Add or subtract with a calculator. *Remember:* The term (OPP) means
"use the opposite of the number."

3. −26 − 17 = _____

   −26 + (OPP) 17 = _____

4. −34 − 68 = _____

   −34 + (−68) = _____

5. 56 − 24 = _____

   56 + (OPP) 24 = _____

6. 18 − 84 = _____

   18 + (−84) = _____

7. 43 − (−97) = _____

   43 + (OPP) (−97) = _____

   43 + 97 = _____

8. 31 − (−13) = _____

   31 + (−(−13)) = _____

   31 + 13 = _____

9. −130 − (−62) = _____

   −130 + (OPP) (−62) = _____

   −130 + 62 = _____

10. −2 − (−22) = _____

    −2 + (−(−22)) = _____

    −2 + 22 = _____

Use with Lesson 6.3.

Subtracting Positive and Negative Numbers

One way to subtract one number from another number is to change
the subtraction problem into an addition problem.

> **Subtraction Rule**
> To subtract a number *b* from a number *a*, add the opposite of *b* to *a*.
> Thus, for any numbers *a* and *b*, $a - b = a + (OPP)\ b$, or $a - b = a + (-b)$.

Examples

$6 - 9 = 6 + (OPP)\ 9 = 6 + (-9) = -3$
$-15 - (-23) = -15 + (OPP)\ (-23) = -15 + 23 = 8$

Rewrite each subtraction problem as an addition problem. Then solve the problem.

1. $22 - (15) =$ _____ $22 + (OPP)\ 15 = 7$_____

2. $-35 - 20 =$ _____

3. $-3 - (-4.5) =$ _____

4. $-27 - (-27) =$ _____

Subtract.

5. $-23 - (-5) =$ _____   **6.** $9 - (-54) =$ _____   **7.** $-\left(\frac{4}{5}\right) - 1\frac{1}{5} =$ _____

8. $\$1.25 - (-\$6.75) =$ _____   **9.** $-76 - (-56) =$ _____   **10.** $-27 - 100 =$ _____

11. Explain how you solved Problem 9. _____

_____

_____

Fill in the missing numbers.

12. _____ $+ 5 = -10$ **13.** _____ $+ (-5) = -10$ **14.** $-9 +$ _____ $= 0$

$-10 - 5 =$ _____ $-10 - (-5) =$ _____ $0 - (-9) =$ _____

15. $16 +$ _____ $= -7$ **16.** $-25 +$ _____ $= 15$ **17.** _____ $+ 13 = -8$

$-7 - 16 =$ _____ $15 - (-25) =$ _____ $-8 - 13 =$ _____

Use with Lesson 6.3.

Math Boxes 6.3

1. You roll 2 six-sided dice. Give the probability of rolling the following totals.

   a. 2 _____   b. 12 _____

   c. 11 _____   d. 7 _____

   e. 0 _____   f. 3 or 4 _____

   g. An even number _____

2. a. Use your Geometry Template to draw sectors of this spinner and color them so that the chances of landing on these colors are as follows:

   red: 1 out of 4

   blue: $\frac{3}{8}$

   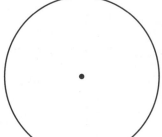

   b. On this spinner, what is the chance of *not* landing on red or blue? _____

3. The distance from Chicago to Los Angeles is about 2,060 miles. A family drove this distance in 4 days. On average, about how many miles did the family travel each day?

   _____

4. Write a mixed number for each fraction.

   a. $\frac{320}{25} =$ _____

   b. _____ $= \frac{43}{7}$

   c. _____ $= \frac{101}{5}$

   d. _____ $= \frac{75}{8}$

   e. $\frac{147}{4} =$ _____

5. Circle the number sentence that describes the numbers in the table.

   $p = m * 2$

   $(3 - m) = p + 8$

   $p = (3 * m) - 8$

   $m - 8 = p$

m	p
8	16
0	-8
4	4
10	22

6. Write each number using digits. Then round each number to the nearest ten-thousand.

   a. Four million, three hundred seventy-two thousand, nine hundred five

   number _____

   rounded _____

   b. Thirteen million, sixty-eight thousand, four hundred twenty-three

   number _____

   rounded _____

Multiplication Patterns

In each of Problems 1–4, complete the patterns in Part a. Check your answers
with a calculator. Then circle the word in parentheses that correctly completes
the statement in Part b.

1. a. $6 * 4 = 24$
        $6 * 3 = 18$
        $6 * 2 =$ _____
        $6 * 1 =$ _____
        $6 * 0 =$ _____

    b. **Positive * Positive Rule:**

        When a positive number
        is multiplied by a positive
        number, the product is a

        (positive or negative) number.

2. a. $5 * 2 = 10$
            $5 * 1 = 5$
            $5 * 0 = 0$
        $5 * (-1) =$ _____
        $5 * (-2) =$ _____

    b. **Positive * Negative Rule:**

        When a positive number
        is multiplied by a negative
        number, the product is a

        (positive or negative) number.

3. a. $2 * 3 = 6$
         $1 * 3 = 3$
         $0 * 3 = 0$
        $-1 * 3 =$ _____
        $-2 * 3 =$ _____

    b. **Negative * Positive Rule:**

        When a negative number
        is multiplied by a positive
        number, the product is a

        (positive or negative) number.

4. a. $-4 * 1 = -4$
            $-4 * 0 = 0$
        $-4 * (-1) = 4$
        $-4 * (-2) =$ _____
        $-4 * (-3) =$ _____

    b. **Negative * Negative Rule:**

        When a negative number
        is multiplied by a negative
        number, the product is a

        (positive or negative) number.

5. a. Solve.
            $-1 * 6 =$ _____
        $-1 * (-7.7) =$ _____
        $-1 * -(-\frac{1}{2}) =$ _____
            $-1 * m =$ _____

    b. **Multiplication Property of −1:**
        For any number a,
        $-1 * a = a * -1 = $ (OPP) a, or $-a$. Since the
        number a can be a negative number, (OPP) a
        or $-a$ can be a positive number. For example,
        if $a = -5$, then $-a = $ (OPP) $-5 = 5$.

Use with Lesson 6.4.

Fact Families for Multiplication and Division

A fact family is a group of four basic, related multiplication and division facts.

Example The multiplication and division fact family for $6 * 3 = 18$ $18 / 6 = 3$
              6, 3, and 18 is made up of the following facts: $3 * 6 = 18$ $18 / 3 = 6$

As you already know, when a positive number is divided by a positive number, the quotient is a positive number. Problems 1 and 2 will help you discover the rules for division with negative numbers. Complete the fact families. Check your answers with a calculator. Then complete each rule.

1. **a.** $5 * (-3) =$ _____   **b.** $6 * (-8) =$ _____   **c.** $5 * (-5) =$ _____

   $-3 * 5 =$ _____ $-8 * 6 =$ _____   _____

   $-15 / (-3) =$ _____ $-48 / (-8) =$ _____   _____

   $-15 / 5 =$ _____ $-48 / 6 =$ _____   _____

   d. **Negative / Negative Rule:**   **e.** **Negative / Positive Rule:**
   When a negative number   When a negative number
   is divided by a negative   is divided by a positive
   number, the quotient is a   number, the quotient is a

   (positive or negative) number.   (positive or negative) number.

2. **a.** $-4 * (-3) =$ _____   **b.** $-7 * (-5) =$ _____   **c.** $-2 * (-10) =$ _____

   $-3 * (-4) =$ _____   _____   _____

   $12 / (-3) =$ _____   _____   _____

   $12 / (-4) =$ _____   _____   _____

   d. **Positive / Negative Rule:**
   When a positive number
   is divided by a negative
   number, the quotient is a

   (positive or negative) number.

3. Solve. Check your answers with a calculator.

   a. _____ $* (-4) = 24$ (*Think:* What number multiplied by -4 is equal to 24?)

   b. _____ $* 9 = -81$ **c.** $-6 *$ _____ $= 48$ **d.** _____ $* (-3) = -27$

   e. $-81 / 9 =$ _____   **f.** $48 / (-6) =$ _____   **g.** $-27 / (-3) =$ _____

*, / of Positive and Negative Numbers

Multiplication Property	Division Property
For all numbers *a* and *b,* if the values of *a* and *b* are both positive or both negative, then the product $a * b$ is a positive number. If one of the values is positive and the other is negative, then the product $a * b$ is a negative number.	For all numbers *a* and *b,* if the values of *a* and *b* are both positive or both negative, then the quotient a / b is a positive number. If one of the values is positive and the other is negative, then the quotient a / b is a negative number.

Solve. Use a calculator to check your answers.

1. $-7 * 8 =$ _____

2. $73 * (-45) =$ _____

3. _____ $\div (-10) = 70$

4. $\frac{1}{2} * (-\frac{3}{4}) =$ _____

5. $0.5 * (-15) =$ _____

6. _____ $* 3.3 = -3.3$

7. $-3 * 4 * (-7) =$ _____

8. _____ $* (-8) * (-3) = -48$

9. $-54 / 9 =$ _____

10. $36 / (-12) =$ _____

11. $-\frac{3}{5} \div (-\frac{4}{5}) =$ _____

12. $45 / (-5) / (-3) =$ _____

13. _____ $\div 15 = -6$

14. $72 / (-8) =$ _____

15. $-99 /$ _____ $= -11$

16. $\frac{1}{2} \div (-\frac{3}{4}) =$ _____

17. $-3 * (-4 + 6) =$ _____

18. $32 \div (-5 - 3) =$ _____

19. $(-9 * 4) + 6 =$ _____

20. $(-75 / 5) + (-20) =$ _____

21. $(-6 * 3) + (-6 * 5) =$ _____

22. $(4 * (-7)) - (4 * (-3)) =$ _____

Evaluate each expression for $y = -4$.

23. $3 - (-y) =$ _____

24. $-y / (-6) =$ _____

25. $y - (-7 + 3) =$ _____

26. $y - (y + 2) =$ _____

27. $(-8 * y) - 6 =$ _____

28. $(-8 * 6) - (-8 * y) =$ _____

Math Boxes 6.4

---

1. Write a percent for each fraction.

a. $\frac{10}{50} =$ _____

b. $\frac{6}{9} =$ _____

c. $\frac{15}{18} =$ _____

d. $\frac{14}{16} =$ _____

e. $\frac{10}{15} =$ _____

---

2. I am a 3-dimensional geometric shape. I have 5 faces. Two faces are triangles. The other faces are rectangles.

I am called a

_____.

---

3. Add or subtract.

a. $3\frac{8}{9} + 1\frac{3}{12} =$ _____

b. $\frac{18}{6} - 1\frac{2}{3} =$ _____

c. $\frac{9}{5} + 4\frac{3}{10} =$ _____

d. $4\frac{5}{8} - 2\frac{7}{12} =$ _____

---

4. Write the reciprocal.

a. 5 _____

b. $\frac{2}{3}$ _____

c. $2\frac{4}{7}$ _____

d. 0.8 _____

e. 9.64 _____

---

5. Estimate each product by rounding the larger factor to the nearest million.

a. $46,882,003 * 4$ _____

b. $831,247 * 27$ _____

c. $3,589,221 * 15$ _____

d. $20 * 13,402,655$ _____

---

6. Divide.

a. $9\overline{)681}$ b. $23\overline{)8,041}$

Scavenger Hunt

Use *Student Reference Book* pages 1–24 and 91–104 to find answers to as many of these questions as you can. Try to get as high a score as possible.

1. How many rational numbers are there? (10 points) _____

2. Give an example of each of the following. (5 points each)

   a. A counting number _____

   b. A negative rational number _____

   c. A positive rational number _____

   d. A real number _____

   e. An integer _____

   f. An irrational number _____

3. Name two examples of uses of negative rational numbers. (5 points each)

   _____

   _____

4. Explain why numbers like 4, $\frac{3}{5}$, and 3.5 are rational numbers. (10 points)

   _____

   _____

   _____

5. Explain why numbers like π and $\sqrt{2}$ are irrational numbers. (10 points)

   _____

6. $n + n = n$ What is n? _____ (15 points)

7. $k = (OPP) k$ What is k? _____ (15 points)

8. $j * j = j$ Which two numbers could j be? _____ (15 points each)

9. $a + (-a) =$ _____ (15 points)   10. $b * \frac{1}{b} =$ _____ (15 points)

Scavenger Hunt (cont.)

11. Match each sentence in Column 1 with the property in Column 2 that it illustrates.
    (5 points each)

Column 1

A. $a + (b + c) = (a + b) + c$

B. $a + b = b + a$

C. $a * (b + c) = (a * b) + (a * c)$

D. $a * (b - c) = (a * b) - (a * c)$

E. $a * b = b * a$

F. $a * (b * c) = (a * b) * c$

Column 2

_____ Distributive property of multiplication over subtraction

_____ Commutative property of addition

_____ Distributive property of multiplication over addition

_____ Associative property of multiplication

_____ Commutative property of multiplication

_____ Associative property of addition

12. $-a > 0$. How can that be? (15 points)

_____

_____

13. Complete. (2 points each, except the last problem, which is worth 25 points)

(OPP) 1 = _____

(OPP) (OPP) 1 = _____

(OPP) (OPP) (OPP) 1 = _____

(OPP) (OPP) (OPP) (OPP) 1 = _____

(OPP) (OPP) (OPP) (OPP) (OPP) 1 = _____

(OPP) (OPP) (OPP) (OPP) (OPP) (OPP) 1 = _____

(OPP) (OPP) (OPP) (OPP) (OPP) (OPP) ... (OPP) (OPP) 1 = _____

100 (OPP)s

Explain how you found the answer to the last problem. _____

_____

_____

Scavenger Hunt (cont.)

14. Is 5^{-2} a positive or negative number? Explain. (15 points)

_____

_____

_____

15. Two numbers are their own reciprocals. What are they? _____ (15 points each)

16. What number has no reciprocal? _____ (15 points)

Number Stories

1. Diana wants to make a 15'-by-20' section of her yard into a garden. She will plant flowers in $\frac{2}{3}$ of the garden and vegetables in the rest of the garden. How many square feet of vegetable garden will she have?

   _____

   Explain how you got your answer. _____

   _____

   _____

   _____

2. Leo is in charge of buying hot dogs for family math night. Out of 300 people, he expects about $\frac{3}{5}$ of them to attend. Hot dogs come 8 to a package, and Leo figures he will need to buy 22 packages so that each person can get 1 hot dog.

   a. How do you think he calculated to get 22 packages?

   _____

   _____

   _____

   b. What was Leo's mistake? _____

   _____

Use with Lesson 6.5.

Math Boxes 6.5

1. Add or subtract.

   a. $2\frac{2}{5} - \frac{8}{10} =$ _____

   b. $\frac{16}{8} - 1\frac{1}{9} =$ _____

   c. $\frac{14}{16} + 2\frac{1}{2} =$ _____

   d. $1\frac{7}{8} + \frac{24}{16} =$ _____

SRB
80 81

2. Complete each sentence with an algebraic expression.

   a. If Mark earns x dollars per hour when he baby-sits, then he earns

   _____ dollars when he baby-sits for $3\frac{1}{2}$ hours.

   b. Bill's dog is 3 years older than his cat. If the dog is y years old, then the cat is

   _____ years old.

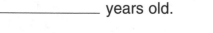

SRB
222

3. Write the following numbers with words.

   a. 249.2 _____

   _____

   b. 0.432 _____

   _____

   c. 0.00001 _____

   _____

SRB
28

4. Give a rough estimate (a ballpark estimate) for each quotient.

   a. 643.27 ÷ 5 _____

   b. 728.09 ÷ 7 _____

   c. 432.67 ÷ 8 _____

   d. 2,091.05 / 5 _____

   e. 324.6 / 4 _____

SRB
50 243

5. Divide.

   a. $\frac{8}{9} \div \frac{3}{4} =$ _____

   b. $\frac{7}{8} \div \frac{1}{3} =$ _____

   c. $\frac{6}{9} \div \frac{1}{2} =$ _____

   d. $\frac{2}{4} \div \frac{3}{8} =$ _____

   e. $\frac{8}{24} \div \frac{4}{24} =$ _____

SRB
89 90

Order of Operations

> Please Excuse My Dear Aunt Sally
> Parentheses Exponents Multiplication Division Addition Subtraction

Evaluate each expression. Show your work. Then compare your answers to those of your partner. If you don't agree, check the answers using a calculator.

Easy

1. $4 * 6 + 3 =$ _____

2. $33 - 16 / 4 =$ _____

3. $4 * 7 - (3 + 5) =$ _____

4. $24 / 6 * 4 =$ _____

Moderate

5. $7 - 5 + 13 - 23 - 17 =$ _____

6. $12 * 2^2 - 3^3 =$ _____

7. $7 / 7 * 4 + 3^2 =$ _____

8. $5 - 15 + 3 * 2 =$ _____

Order of Operations (cont.)

Difficult

9. $10^{-1} + 16 - 0.5 * 12 = $ _____

10. $((\frac{1}{2} \div \frac{1}{4}) + 3) * 6 - 3^3 = $ _____

11. $-(-8) - (-4) * 6 - (-12) / 4 = $ _____

12. $-4 + (-18) / 6 + (-3 * -3 - 5) = $ _____

Challenge

13. $-5(-6 - (-3)) / 7.5 = $ _____

14. $-(\frac{3}{4} \div \frac{1}{2}) + \frac{1}{2} - (\frac{1}{2} * (-\frac{1}{2})) = $ _____

15. Evaluate the following expressions for $x = -2$.

    a. $x * -x + 14 / 2 = $ _____

    b. $-x * (6 + x) - 3^3 / 9 = $ _____

Fraction Number Stories

Write a number model for each problem. Then solve it.

1. Luis figures that one person can eat about $\frac{3}{8}$ of a large pizza.
   How many people can he serve with 6 large pizzas?

   Number model _____   Solution _____

2. Amelia makes rock candy and sells it in $\frac{1}{2}$-pound packages.
   How many packages can she make from 15 pounds of rock candy?

   Number model _____   Solution _____

3. Ian worked 20 minutes cutting the grass and was only $\frac{1}{3}$ finished.
   How long will the whole job take?

   Number model _____   Solution _____

Write a number story to fit each of these number models.

4. $5 \div \frac{1}{2} = n$

   _____

   _____

   _____

   Solution _____

5. $12 \div \frac{2}{3} = k$

   _____

   _____

   _____

   Solution _____

Use with Lesson 6.6.

Math Boxes 6.6

1. Complete.

a. $\frac{1}{8}$ of 2 = _____

b. $\frac{3}{4}$ of 80 = _____

c. $\frac{4}{7}$ of 77 = _____

d. $\frac{1}{2}$ of $\frac{1}{8}$ = _____

e. $\frac{5}{12}$ of 60 = _____

SRB
83 85

2. Alan bought a model car for $8.98, a pair of shoes for $14.49, and a new jacket for $24.95. How much more did he spend on the jacket than on the model car?

_____

SRB
239

3. Add or subtract.

a. $32 + (-52)$ = _____

b. _____ = $16 - 29$

c. _____ = $48 - (-63)$

d. _____ = $-56 + 94$

e. $-28 - (-43)$ = _____

SRB
92 93

4. Draw a 72° angle. Label the angle.

Circle the kind of angle you drew.

acute   obtuse   reflex   right   straight

SRB
148
212–214

5. Complete the table. Then graph the data and connect the points.

Heather earns $0.35 for each paper flower she makes for the school fun fair.

Flowers (f)	Earnings ($) (0.35 * f)
1	
2	
	1.05
5	
	2.10

Rule: Earnings = $0.35 * number of flowers

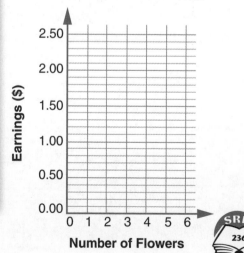

Heather's Earnings

Earnings ($) / Number of Flowers

Number Sentences

Translate the word sentences below into number sentences. Study the first one.

1. Three times five is equal to fifteen. _____ $3 * 5 = 15$ _____

2. Nine increased by seven is less than twenty-nine. _____

3. Thirteen is not equal to nine more than twenty. _____

4. The product of eight and six is less than or equal to the sum of twenty and thirty.

   _____

5. Thirty-seven increased by twelve is greater than fifty decreased by ten.

   _____

6. Nineteen is less than or equal to nineteen. _____

Tell whether each number sentence is true or false.

7. $3 * 21 = 63$ _____   8. $(3 * 4) + 7 = 19$ _____

9. $42 - 12 / 6 > 5$ _____   10. $8 \geq 7 + 1$ _____

11. $24 / 4 + 2 = 8$ _____   12. $9 / (8 - 5) \leq 3$ _____

13. $21 > (7 * 3) + 5$ _____   14. $8 * 7 \leq 72$ _____

15. $63 / 7 \neq 8$ _____   16. $35 + 5 * 8 = 320$ _____

Insert parentheses so that each number sentence is true.

17. $5 * 8 + 4 - 2 = 42$ 18. $7 * 9 - 6 = 21$

19. $10 + 2 * 6 < 24$ 20. $9 - 7 / 7 = 8$

21. $33 - 24 / 3 \geq 25$ 22. $36 / 7 + 2 * 3 = 12$

23. $3 * 4 + 3 > 5 * 3 + 3$ 24. $48 / 8 + 4 \neq 100 / 10$

Use with Lesson 6.7.

Number Sentences (cont.)

25. Write three true and three false number sentences. Trade journals with your partner and determine which sentences are true and which are false.

Number Sentence   **True or false?**

_____   _____

_____   _____

_____   _____

_____   _____

_____   _____

_____   _____

Challenge

26. The word HOPE is printed in block letters inside a 15-foot-by-5-foot rectangular billboard. What is the area of the unshaded portion of the billboard?

_____

27. Square corners, 6 centimeters on a side, are removed from a 36-centimeter-by-42-centimeter piece of paper. The paper is then folded to form an open box. What is the surface area of the inside of the box?

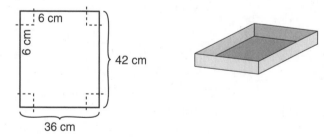

_____

28. Pennies tossed onto the gameboard at the right have an equal chance of landing anywhere on the board. If 60% of the pennies land inside the smaller square, what is the length of a side s of the smaller square, to the nearest inch?

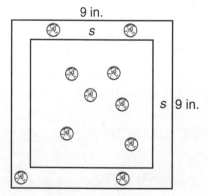

Try the Penny Toss!

_____

Math Boxes 6.7

1. Add or subtract.

   a. $\frac{8}{10} + 8\frac{1}{3} =$ _____

   b. $5\frac{4}{5} - 2\frac{7}{8} =$ _____

   c. $\frac{15}{4} + \frac{9}{7} =$ _____

   d. $\frac{23}{10} - 1\frac{1}{5} =$ _____

2. Complete each sentence with an algebraic expression.

   a. If each bag of potatoes weighs at least p pounds, then 6 bags weigh at least

   _____ pounds.

   b. Jack is 6 inches taller than Michael. If Jack is h inches tall, then Michael is

   _____ inches tall.

3. Write the following numbers with words.

   a. 0.001 _____

   b. 0.017 _____

   c. 0.0001 _____

   d. 2.603 _____

4. Give a rough estimate (a ballpark estimate) for each quotient.

   a. 137.8 ÷ 6 _____

   b. 248.19 ÷ 12 _____

   c. 4,507.08 ÷ 9 _____

   d. 26,991.05 / 3 _____

   e. 2,804.79 / 4 _____

5. Divide.

   a. $\frac{5}{6} \div \frac{1}{2} =$ _____

   b. $\frac{3}{8} \div \frac{3}{4} =$ _____

   c. $\frac{2}{3} \div \frac{5}{6} =$ _____

   d. $\frac{20}{25} \div \frac{5}{25} =$ _____

   e. $\frac{7}{12} \div \frac{2}{5} =$ _____

Solving Equations

Find the solution to each equation. Write a number sentence with the solution in place of the variable. Check that the number sentence is true.

Equation	**Solution**	**Number Sentence**
1. $12 + x = 32$	_____	_____
2. $y + 89 = 93$	_____	_____
3. $b - 32 = 15$	_____	_____
4. $m * 8 = 35 - 19$	_____	_____
5. $p + (4 * 9) = 55$	_____	_____
6. $42 = 7 * (a - 4)$	_____	_____
7. $(9 + w) / 2 = 6 + (6 / 6)$	_____	_____
8. $4 + (3n - 6) = 1 + (3 * 6)$	_____	_____

Find the solution to each equation.

9. $4 * 6 = 35 - t$ _____   **10.** $9 * (11 - c) = 81$ _____

11. $17 - 11 = k / 8$ _____   **12.** $(m + 14) / 4 = 6$ _____

13. $36 / 9 = 2 + p$ _____   **14.** $23 - a = 15$ _____

15. $(3 * p) + 5 = 26$ _____   **16.** $2 - d = 3 * 4$ _____

17. Make up four equations whose solutions are whole numbers.
Ask your partner to solve each one.

Equation	**Solution**
a. _____	_____
b. _____	_____
c. _____	_____
d. _____	_____

Math Boxes 6.8

---

1. Complete.

a. $\frac{1}{8}$ of 48 = _____

b. $\frac{5}{9}$ of 90 = _____

c. $\frac{2}{17}$ of 51 = _____

d. $\frac{3}{19}$ of 95 = _____

e. $\frac{8}{10}$ of 800 = _____

2. At a garage sale, Alisha sold her CDs for $29.00, her stuffed dog for $7.65, and her old tricycle for $12.80. How much more did she sell her CDs for than her old tricycle?

_____

---

3. Add or subtract.

a. $25 - (-14) =$ _____

b. _____ $= -18 - 5$

c. _____ $= -74 - (-8)$

d. _____ $= 46 + (-38)$

e. $-87 + 42 =$ _____

4. Draw a 256° angle. Label the angle.

Circle the kind of angle you drew.

acute   obtuse   reflex   right   straight

---

5. Complete the table. Then graph the data and connect the points.

Rebecca walks at an average speed of $3\frac{1}{2}$ miles per hour.

Time (hr) (*h*)	Distance (mi) ($3\frac{1}{2} * h$)
1	
2	
	$17\frac{1}{2}$
7	
	35

Rule: Distance = $3\frac{1}{2}$ miles per hour * number of hours

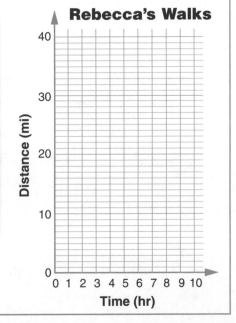

Rebecca's Walks

Use with Lesson 6.8.

Pan-Balance Problems

A pan balance can be used to compare the weights of objects or to weigh objects. If the objects in one pan weigh as much as those in the other pan, the pans will balance.

The diagram at the right shows a balanced pan balance.

Example In each of the diagrams below, the pans are balanced. Your job is to figure out how many marbles weigh as much as an orange. The best way to do this is to move oranges and marbles so that a single orange is in one pan and only marbles are in the other pan. When moving the oranges and marbles, you must follow these simple rules: *Whatever you do, the pans must always remain balanced. You must do the same thing to both pans.*

The pan balance shows that 3 oranges weigh as much as 1 orange and 12 marbles.

If you remove 1 orange from each pan, the pans remain balanced.

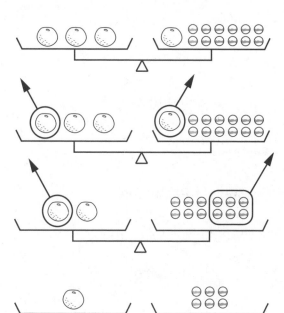

If you then remove half of the objects from each pan, the pans will still be balanced.

Success! One orange weighs as much as 6 marbles.

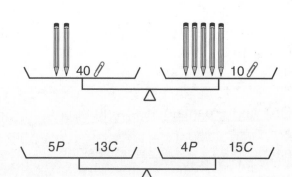

Solve the pan-balance problems with a partner. Be ready to share your strategies with the class.

1. One pencil weighs as much

   as _____ paper clips.

2. One *P* (pencil) weighs as much

   as _____ *C*s (paper clips).

Pan-Balance Problems (cont.)

Solve these pan-balance problems. In each figure, the two pans are balanced.

Warm-Up Problems

1. One banana weighs as much

   as _____ marbles.

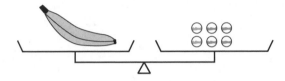

2. One cube weighs as much

   as _____ paper clips.

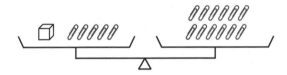

3. One cube weighs as much

   as _____ marbles.

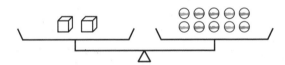

Slightly Sweaty Problems

4. One triangle weighs as much

   as _____ squares.

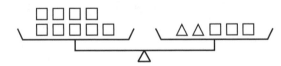

5. One orange weighs as much

   as _____ paper clips.

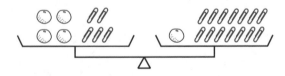

6. One and $\frac{1}{2}$ cantaloupes weigh

   as much as _____ apples.

Use with Lesson 6.9.

Pan-Balance Problems (cont.)

Reminder: $4 \square$ or $4 * \square$ is just another way to write $\square + \square + \square + \square$.

Heart-Rate-Is-Really-Soaring-Now Problems

7. One cube weighs as much

   as _____ coins.

8. One *P* weighs as

   much as _____ balls.

9. One *B* weighs

   as much as _____ *K*s.

10. One *X* weighs

   as much as _____ *Y*s.

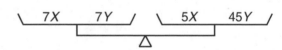

Check your answers.

- The sum of the answers to Problems 1 and 4 is equal to the square root of 81.

- The answer to Problem 10 is a prime number greater than 17 and less than 5^2.

- The product of the answers to Problems 6 and 7 is 36.

- The sum of the answers to Problems 1 and 10 is the solution to the equation $4n = 10^2$.

- The product of the answers to Problems 5, 7, and 9 is 24.

Math Boxes 6.9

1. Complete the table.

Fraction	Decimal	Percent
$\frac{5}{8}$		
	0.65	
		47%
$\frac{8}{12}$		

2. Multiply or divide.

a. $-3 * 5 = $ _____

b. $-10 * -8 = $ _____

c. _____ $= -4 * -30$

d. _____ $= 28 \div -7$

e. _____ $= -56 \div -8$

3. Use the following formula to calculate about how long it will take an object to reach the bottom of a well:

$$t = \frac{1}{4} * \sqrt{d}$$

where d is the distance in feet the object falls and t is the time in seconds it takes to reach the bottom. This formula does not account for air resistance. About how long would it take a bowling ball to hit the bottom of a well 100 feet deep?

_____

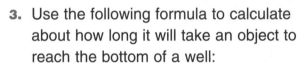

4. Tell what additional information you need to solve the following problem: Melissa took 3 friends to lunch. She had $20 to spend on lunch. All 4 people ordered spaghetti. How much change did Melissa receive from her $20?

_____

_____

_____

5. Make each sentence true by inserting parentheses.

a. $4 * 7 - 6 / 3 = 26$

b. $3^3 - 49 / 7 + 12 = 8$

c. $2\frac{5}{8} - 3 / 4 + 1 / 2 = 2\frac{3}{8}$

d. $6 + 15 / 3 - 2 * 5 = 1$

e. $2\frac{5}{8} - 3 / 4 + 1 / 2 = 1\frac{3}{8}$

     Use with Lesson 6.9.

Math Boxes 6.10

---

1. Multiply. Write your answers in simplest form.

a. $\frac{3}{8} * \frac{2}{5} =$ _____

b. $\frac{6}{10} * \frac{7}{8} =$ _____

c. _____ $= \frac{2}{3} * \frac{9}{11}$

d. _____ $= \frac{4}{12} * \frac{5}{3}$

e. _____ $= \frac{7}{8} * \frac{5}{6}$

2. Write > or < to make each sentence true.

a. $\frac{5}{8}$ _____ $\frac{3}{16}$

b. $\frac{4}{7}$ _____ $\frac{5}{6}$

c. $1\frac{1}{8}$ _____ $\frac{9}{7}$

d. $\frac{10}{11}$ _____ $\frac{8}{9}$

e. $\frac{15}{12}$ _____ $\frac{16}{15}$

---

3. Multiply.

a.   64.8
   $*$ 12.9

b.   22.04
   $*$ 48.7

c.   3.16
   $*$ 29.2

---

4. Give this mystery graph a title, label the axes, and describe a situation it might represent.

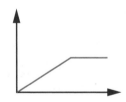

_____

_____

_____

_____

5. Complete.

a. $16\frac{2}{3}\%$ of 36 = _____

b. $33\frac{1}{3}\%$ of 54 = _____

c. 75% of 88 = _____

d. 59% of 100 = _____

e. $12\frac{1}{2}\%$ of 48 = _____

Pan-Balance Equations

1. Start with the original pan-balance equation. Do the first operation on both sides of the pan balance, and write the result on the second pan balance. Do the second operation on both sides of the second pan balance, and write the result on the third pan balance. Fill in the fourth pan balance in the same way.

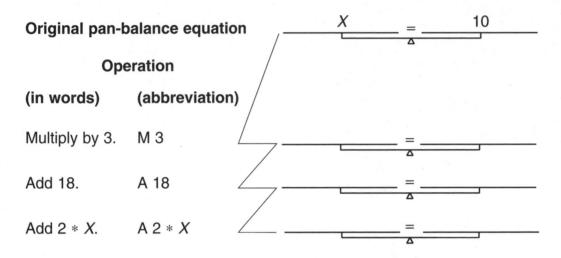

Original pan-balance equation

Operation

(in words)   **(abbreviation)**

Multiply by 3.   M 3

Add 18.   A 18

Add 2 * X.   A 2 * X

Equations that have the same solution are called **equivalent equations.**

2. Check that the pan-balance equations above are equivalent equations (that is, that 10 is the solution to each equation).

3. Now do the opposite of what you did in Problem 1. Record on each pan balance the operation used to obtain the results.

Original pan-balance equation $(5 * X) + 18 \ = \ (2 * X) + 48$

Operation

(in words)   **(abbreviation)**

_____   _____ $(3 * X) + 18 \ = \ 48$

_____   _____ $3 * X \ = \ 30$

_____   _____ $X \ = \ 10$

Pan-Balance Equations (cont.)

4. Record the results of the operation on each pan, as in Problem 1.

Original pan-balance equation

      Operation

(in words)   **(abbreviation)**

Subtract 2.   S 2

Multiply by 4.   M 4

Add 2n.   A 2n

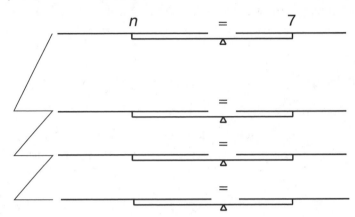

5. Check that the solution to each pan-balance equation in Problem 4 is 7.

In Problems 6 and 7, record the operation that was used to obtain the results onto each pan balance, as you did in Problem 3.

6. Original pan-balance equation

             Operation

(in words)   **(abbreviation)**

_____   _____

_____   _____

_____   _____

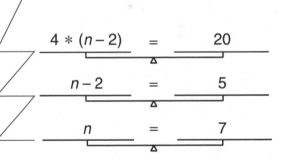

7. Original pan-balance equation

          Operation

(in words)   **(abbreviation)**

_____   _____

_____   _____

_____   _____

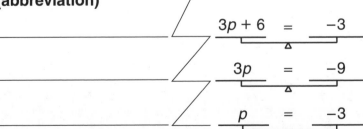

8. Check that 7 is the solution to each pan-balance equation in Problem 6 and that -3 is the solution to each pan-balance equation in Problem 7.

Inventing and Solving Equations

Work in groups of three. Each of you will invent two equations and then ask the other two group members to solve them. You will show your solutions on page 243. Here is what you should do for each equation.

Step 1 Choose any positive or negative integer and record it on the first line to complete the original equation.

Step 2 Apply any operation you wish to both sides of the equation. Record the operation and write the new (equivalent) equation on the lines below the original equation.

Step 3 Repeat Step 2. Apply a new operation and show the new equation that results.

Step 4 Check your work by substituting the original value of x in each equation you have written. You should get a true number sentence every time.

Step 5 Give the other members of your group the final equation to solve.

1. Make up an equation from two equivalent equations.   Selected integer

Original equation _____ x _____ = _____

Operation

_____ _____ = _____

_____ _____ = _____

2. Make up an equation from three equivalent equations.   Selected integer

Original equation _____ x _____ = _____

Operation

_____ _____ = _____

_____ _____ = _____

_____ _____ = _____

Inventing and Solving Equations (cont.)

Use this page to solve your partners' equations.

First, record the equation. Then solve it. For each step, record the operation you use and the equation that results. Check your solution by substituting it for the variable in your partners' equation. Finally, compare the steps you used to solve your partners' equation to the steps your partners used in inventing the equation.

1. Partners' equation _____ = _____

Operation

_____ _____ = _____

_____ _____ = _____

_____ _____ = _____

2. Partners' equation _____ = _____

Operation

_____ _____ = _____

_____ _____ = _____

_____ _____ = _____

3. Partners' equation _____ = _____

Operation

_____ _____ = _____

_____ _____ = _____

_____ _____ = _____

4. Partners' equation _____ = _____

Operation

_____ _____ = _____

_____ _____ = _____

_____ _____ = _____

Solving Equations

Solve the following equations.

Example

$3x + 5 = 14$

Original equation $3x + 5 = 14$

Operation

S 5	$3x = 9$
D 3	$x = 3$

Check $(3 * 3) + 5 = 14$; true

1. $11y - 4 = 9y$

Original equation

_____

Operation

_____   _____

_____   _____

_____   _____

Check _____

---

2. $16t + 7 = 19t + 10$

Original equation

_____

Operation

_____   _____

_____   _____

_____   _____

Check _____

3. $12n - 5 = 9n - 2$

Original equation

_____

Operation

_____   _____

_____   _____

_____   _____

Check _____

---

4. $8k - 6 = 10k + 6$

Original equation

_____

Operation

_____   _____

_____   _____

_____   _____

Check _____

5. $3b + 7.1 = 2.5b + 11.5$

Original equation

_____

Operation

_____   _____

_____   _____

_____   _____

Check _____

Use with Lesson 6.11.

Solving Equations (cont.)

6. $8 - 3h = 5h + 1$

Original equation

_____

Operation

_____   _____

_____   _____

_____   _____

Check _____

7. $-2p - 6 = 12 - 4p$

Original equation

_____

Operation

_____   _____

_____   _____

_____   _____

Check _____

8. $\frac{1}{4}r + 9 = 10 - \frac{3}{4}r$

Original equation

_____

Operation

_____   _____

_____   _____

Check _____

9. $\frac{2}{3}u - 7 = 9 - \frac{2}{3}u$

Original equation

_____

Operation

_____   _____

_____   _____

_____   _____

Check _____

Challenge

Two equations are equivalent if they have the same solution. Circle each pair of equivalent equations. Write the solution to the equations if the equations are equivalent.

10. $z = 5$

$3z - 8 = 2z - 3$

Solution _____

11. $d + 5 = 8$

$6 - 2d = 9 - 3d$

Solution _____

12. $v + 1 = 2v + 2$

$3v - 8 = 2v - 3$

Solution _____

13. $t = 4$

$(5t + 3) - 2(t + 3) = 29 - 5t$

Solution _____

Use with Lesson 6.11.

Math Boxes 6.11

1. Complete the table.

Fraction	Decimal	Percent
$\frac{15}{20}$		
	0.9	
		24%
	0.35	

2. Multiply or divide.

a. $-3 * -12 =$ _____

b. $-50 * 70 =$ _____

c. _____ $= -200 * -500$

d. _____ $* 70 = -630$

e. _____ $* -40 = 1,600$

3. Suppose N is a 2-digit whole number that ends in 5, such as 15. It is easy to calculate the square of N by using the formula

$$N^2 = (t * (t + 1) * 100) + 25$$

where t is the tens digit of the number you are squaring. Use this formula to find the following. (*Hint:* In Problem a, $t = 3$.)

a. $35^2 =$ _____

b. $75^2 =$ _____

c. $95^2 =$ _____

4. Tell what additional information you need to solve the following problem:
Sam has 2 baseball cards that are worth $4.20 each and 3 baseball cards that are worth $7 each. The rest of his cards are worth $1 each. How much is his collection worth in all?

_____

_____

_____

_____

5. Make each sentence true by inserting parentheses.

a. $4 * 7 - 6 / 3 = \frac{4}{3}$

b. $3^2 - 38 / 7 + 12 = 7$

c. $2\frac{5}{8} - 3 / 4 - 1 + 1 / 2 = 2\frac{1}{8}$

d. $6 + 15 / 3 - 2 * 5 = 1$

e. $18 / 3^2 - 6 + 8 = 14$

Use with Lesson 6.11.

Introduction to Inequalities

1. Translate each inequality into an English sentence.

   a. $15 \neq 3 * 7$ _____ *15 is not equal to 3 times 7.* _____

   b. $(9 / 9) + 13 \leq 14$ _____

   _____

   c. $7 > 1 * \frac{2}{3}$ _____

   _____

   d. $23 < 6 * 3$ _____

   _____

   e. $20 \geq 5^2$ _____

   _____

2. Are all of the inequalities in Problem 1 true? _____

   If not, which are false? _____

3. Some of the inequalities below are true, and some are false.
   Write "true" or "false" after each one.

   a. $5 * 4 < 20$ _____   b. $(7 + 3) * 6 \neq 60$ _____

   c. $54 / 9 > 7$ _____   d. $9 - (3 * 2) < 10$ _____

   e. $45 \geq 9 * 5$ _____   f. $3 \leq -1 + 6$ _____

   g. $15 \leq 12 + 2$ _____   h. $17 - 6 \geq 9$ _____

4. a. Write an inequality that is neither true nor false.

   _____

   b. Explain how you can change it into an inequality that is true.

   _____

   _____

Date _____   Time _____

Inequalities

1. Name two solutions for each inequality.

    a. $15 > r$ _____   **b.** $8 < m$ _____

    c. $t \geq 56$ _____   **d.** $15 - 11 \leq p$ _____

    e. $\frac{21}{7} \geq y$ _____   **f.** $w > -3$ _____

    g. $6.5 \geq 3 * d$ _____   **h.** $g \leq 0.5$ _____

2. Name two numbers that are *not* solutions to each inequality.

    a. $(7 + 3) * q \geq 40$ _____   **b.** $\frac{1}{2} + \frac{1}{4} < t$ _____

    c. $y \leq 2.6 + 4.3$ _____   **d.** $6 / g > 12$ _____

3. Describe the solution set to each inequality.

    Example $t + 5 < 8$

    Solution set: All numbers less than 3

    a. $8 - y > 3$ Solution set _____

    b. $4b \geq 8$ Solution set _____

4. Graph the solution set to each inequality.

    a. $x < 5$

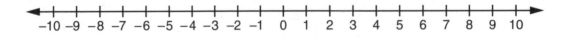

    b. $6 > b$

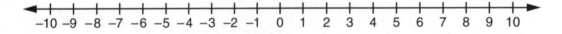

    c. $1\frac{1}{2} \geq h$

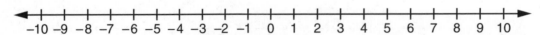

         Use with Lesson 6.12.

Operations with Positive and Negative Numbers

1. $17 - (-17) =$ _____

2. $-24 + 50 =$ _____

3. $-43 - (-21) =$ _____

4. $34 + (-75) =$ _____

5. **a.** Is the answer to Problem 2 positive or negative? _____

b. Why? _____

_____

_____

_____

_____

6. $20 * (-8) =$ _____

7. $-6 * (-15) =$ _____

8. $48 \div (-6) =$ _____

9. $-81 \div (-9) =$ _____

10. $-35 \div (-7) =$ _____

11. $-7 * 50 =$ _____

12. **a.** Is the answer to Problem 7 positive or negative? _____

b. Why? _____

_____

_____

_____

_____

Use order of operations to solve the problems below.

13. $-5 * 3 + 24 - 4 * 8 =$ _____

14. $23 + 15 * 2 - (-6)^2 =$ _____

Math Boxes 6.12

---

1. Multiply. Write your answer in simplest form.

a. $\frac{7}{9} * \frac{2}{3} = $ _____

b. $\frac{5}{6} * \frac{4}{10} = $ _____

c. _____ $= \frac{4}{5} * \frac{5}{7}$

d. _____ $= \frac{4}{3} * \frac{10}{15}$

e. _____ $= \frac{8}{12} * \frac{7}{9}$

2. Write > or < to make each sentence true.

a. $\frac{5}{9}$ _____ $\frac{6}{10}$

b. $\frac{7}{12}$ _____ $\frac{8}{15}$

c. $\frac{15}{8}$ _____ $1\frac{6}{7}$

d. $\frac{11}{12}$ _____ $\frac{8}{9}$

e. $\frac{4}{7}$ _____ $\frac{5}{9}$

---

3. Multiply.

a.   42.6
      $* \ 38.15$

b.   12.7
      $* \ 60.3$

c.   80.2
      $* \ 4.3$

---

4. Give this mystery graph a title, label the axes, and describe a situation it might represent.

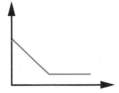

_____

_____

_____

_____

_____

5. Complete.

a. 80% of 50 = _____

b. 10% of 83 = _____

c. 25% of 48 = _____

d. 35% of 100 = _____

e. 50% of 72 = _____

Time to Reflect

1. In this unit, you have been studying algebra concepts and practicing algebra skills. How would you explain to someone what algebra is?

_____

_____

_____

_____

2. Explain why $3 + x$ is not a number sentence but $15 > 9$ is a number sentence.

_____

_____

_____

_____

3. Why do you think patterns were used to introduce the rules for multiplying and dividing signed numbers?

_____

_____

_____

_____

4. Which properties of numbers and number systems did you learn about in this unit?

_____

_____

_____

_____

Math Boxes 6.13

1. The following table shows the results of rolling a six-sided die 50 times.

Number Showing	1	2	3	4	5	6
Number of Times	10	5	11	12	4	8

Tell whether each sentence below is true or false.

a. On the next roll of the die, a 5 is more likely to come up than a 1. _____

b. There is a 50-50 chance of rolling a prime number. _____

c. There is a 50-50 chance of rolling a composite number. _____

---

2. Multiply. Write your answer in simplest form.

a. $\dfrac{6}{8} * \dfrac{2}{5} =$ _____

b. $\dfrac{3}{9} * \dfrac{9}{12} =$ _____

c. _____ $= \dfrac{4}{7} * \dfrac{6}{5}$

d. _____ $= \dfrac{8}{10} * \dfrac{30}{47}$

e. _____ $= \dfrac{7}{25} * \dfrac{75}{100}$

---

3. Rewrite each fraction as a percent.

a. $\dfrac{20}{40} =$ _____

b. $\dfrac{35}{50} =$ _____

c. $\dfrac{18}{24} =$ _____

d. $\dfrac{7}{8} =$ _____

e. $\dfrac{15}{75} =$ _____

---

4. Add.

a. $\dfrac{3}{8} + 1\dfrac{3}{4} =$ _____

b. $\dfrac{2}{3} + 5\dfrac{1}{5} =$ _____

c. $\dfrac{7}{8} + \dfrac{2}{4} + \dfrac{1}{3} =$ _____

d. $\dfrac{3}{5} + \dfrac{3}{8} =$ _____

e. $\dfrac{2}{9} + 2\dfrac{1}{3} =$ _____

---

5. Solve.

a. $\dfrac{4}{7}$ of 56 = _____

b. $\dfrac{2}{3}$ of 15 = _____

c. $\dfrac{8}{9}$ of 72 = _____

d. $\dfrac{3}{8}$ of 32 = _____

e. $\dfrac{9}{10}$ of 31 = _____

Use with Lesson 6.13.

Probability

In a probability experiment, each possible result is called an **outcome.** If each possible result has the *same chance of happening,* the outcomes are **equally likely.**

When you roll a fair 6-sided die, each of the numbers from 1 to 6 has an equal chance of coming up: The possible outcomes are 1, 2, 3, 4, 5, and 6. This fact does *not* mean that in six rolls each number will come up exactly once. A 2 might come up three times; a 6 might not come up at all. But in 100 rolls, each number is likely to come up about $\frac{1}{6}$ of the time. In 1,000 rolls, it's even *more* likely that each number will come up about $\frac{1}{6}$ of the time. So, we say that the **probability** of rolling a 1 (or a 2, 3, 4, 5, or 6) is $\frac{1}{6}$.

The spinner at the right has 5 equal parts; two parts are blue. If you spin it often enough, the spinner is likely to land on blue about $\frac{2}{5}$ of the time. The probability of landing on blue is $\frac{2}{5}$, or 40%.

Here are pictures of 6 spinners. Next to each statement below, write the letter of the spinner it describes. A spinner may be matched with more than one statement.

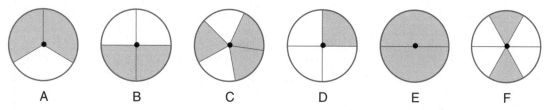

A   B   C   D   E   F

Example This spinner will land on blue about 2 out of 3 times. ___*A*___

1. There is about a $\frac{1}{4}$ chance that this spinner will land on blue. _____

2. This spinner will land on blue 100% of the time. _____

3. There is about a 50-50 chance that this spinner will land on white. _____

4. This spinner will never land on white. _____

5. The probability that this spinner will land on blue is $\frac{3}{5}$. _____

6. This spinner will land on white about twice as often as on blue. _____

7. This spinner will land on white a little less than half of the time. _____

8. The probability that this spinner will land on white is 75%. _____

Domino Probabilities

A set of double-6 dominoes is shown below.

Suppose that all of the dominoes are turned facedown and mixed thoroughly.
You select one domino and turn it faceup.

1. How many possible outcomes are there? _____ possible outcomes

2. Are the outcomes equally likely? _____

When the possible outcomes are equally likely, the following formula is used
to find the probabilities:

$$\text{Probability} = \frac{\text{number of favorable outcomes}}{\text{number of possible outcomes}}$$

3. What is the probability of selecting each domino? _____

Find the probability of selecting each domino described below.

4. A double _____   5. Exactly one blank side _____

6. No blank sides _____   7. The sum of the dots is 7 _____

8. The sum of the dots is greater than 7 _____

9. Exactly one side is a 3 _____

10. Both sides are odd numbers _____

Use with Lesson 7.1.

Math Boxes 7.1

---

1. Solve.

Solution

a. $\dfrac{q}{8} = 16$ _____

b. $\dfrac{60}{p} = 5$ _____

c. $\dfrac{3}{7} = \dfrac{t}{28}$ _____

d. $\dfrac{f}{21} = \dfrac{2}{14}$ _____

SRB
67 68
111

---

2. Fill in the missing equivalents.

Fraction	Decimal	Percent
$\dfrac{7}{8}$		
	0.73	
		30%
	0.625	
$\dfrac{28}{40}$		

SRB
32
36 37

---

3. The area A of a circle is given by the formula $A = \pi * r^2$, where r is the radius of the circle. Use the formula to calculate the area of the circle below.

Area _____
(unit)

SRB
200

---

4. Multiply. Show your work.

a.   46
  * 19

b.   707
  * 32

SRB
19 20

---

5. Write each number in standard notation.

a. 72 billion = _____

b. 0.3 trillion = _____

c. 42.78 million = _____

d. 89.6 billion = _____

e. 0.5 million = _____

SRB
4

---

6. Draw a reflex angle LNE. Then measure it.

Measure of $\angle LNE$ is about _____°.

SRB
148
212–214

Generating Random Numbers

Math Message

Suppose you have a deck of number cards, one card for each of the numbers 1 through 5. When you shuffle the cards and pick a card without looking, you get a number 1 through 5. Each number has the same chance of being picked. Numbers found in this way are **random numbers.**

Suppose you continue finding random numbers using these steps.

- Shuffle
- Pick a card
- Replace the card
- Repeat

1. If you did this many times, about what percent of the time would you expect to pick the number 5?   About _____ percent

---

An Experiment

2. Work with a partner in a group of 4 students. Use a deck of 5 number cards, one card for each of the numbers 1 through 5.

3. One of you shuffles the deck of 5 number cards and fans them out, facedown. Your partner then picks one without looking. The pick **generates a random number** from 1 to 5. The number is an **outcome.**

4. The person picking the card tallies the outcome in the table below while the person with the deck replaces the card and shuffles the deck. Generate exactly 25 random numbers.

Outcome	Tally	Number of Times Picked
1		
2		
3		
4		
5		
Total Random Numbers		25

Use with Lesson 7.2.

Generating Random Numbers (cont.)

5. Record the results in the table below. In the My Partnership column, write the number of times each of the numbers 1 through 5 appeared.

6. In the Other Partnership column, record the results of the other partnership in your group.

7. For each outcome, add the two results and write the sum in the Both Partnerships column.

8. Convert each result under Both Partnerships to a percent. Write it in the % of Total column. (For example, 10 out of 50 would be 20%.)

Outcome	My Partnership	Other Partnership	Both Partnerships	% of Total
1			_____ out of 50	
2			_____ out of 50	
3			_____ out of 50	
4			_____ out of 50	
5			_____ out of 50	
Total	25	25	50 out of 50	100%

Pan-Balances and Equations

Solve the pan-balance problems.

1.

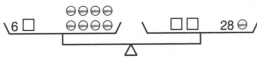

One ☐ weighs as much

as _____ marbles.

2.

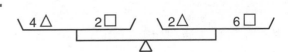

One △ weighs as much

as _____ ☐s.

3.

a. One block weighs as much

    as _____ marbles.

b. One ball weighs as much

    as _____ marbles.

Solve the equations. Show the steps you used to solve each problem.
Check your work.

4. Original equation $8y - 7 = 33$

Problem _____

Operation

_____ _____

_____ _____

Check _____

5. Original equation $3t + 4 = (-59) + 10t$

Problem _____

Operation

_____ _____

_____ _____

_____ _____

Check _____

Math Boxes 7.2

1. Divide.

    a. $8\overline{)1{,}742}$ **b.** $29\overline{)697}$ **c.** $47\overline{)4{,}802}$

SRB
22–24

2. Complete the table for the formula below. Then plot the points to make a graph.

Formula: $2s - 5 = t$

s	t
1	
2	
5	
	11
	15

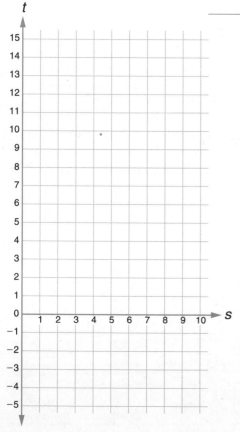

SRB
236

3. The highest point on Earth is the top of Mt. Everest, which is 8,848 meters above sea level. The lowest point on land is the Dead Sea, which is 399 meters below sea level. The lowest point on Earth's surface is thought to be in the Pacific Ocean at 11,034 meters below sea level.

    a. How much higher is the top of Mt. Everest than the Dead Sea?

    _____

                 (unit)

    b. How many more meters below sea level is the lowest point on Earth than the Dead Sea?

    _____

                 (unit)

SRB
91 239

Using Random Numbers

Suppose two evenly matched teams play a game that cannot end in a tie—one team must win. Because the teams have an equal chance of winning, you could get about the same results by randomly generating the numbers 1 and 2: You can do this by tossing a coin. If the coin lands on HEADS, Team 1 wins; if it lands on TAILS, Team 2 wins. In this way, tossing a coin **simulates** the outcome of a game. In a **simulation,** an object or event is represented by something else.

Suppose Team 1 and Team 2 play a "best-of-5" tournament. The first team to win three games wins. The team might win the first three games played; or three of the first four games; or three of five games. Use a coin to simulate the tournament, as follows:

Game 1   If the coin lands on HEADS, Team 1 wins. If the coin lands on TAILS, Team 2 wins.

Games 2 and 3   Repeat the instructions for Game 1.

Games 4 and 5   Play only if necessary. Repeat the instructions for Game 1.

Sample results:

If the coin tosses are HEADS, HEADS, HEADS, Team 1 wins the tournament.

If the coin tosses are HEADS, HEADS, TAILS, HEADS, Team 1 wins.

If the coin tosses are TAILS, HEADS, HEADS, TAILS, TAILS, Team 2 wins.

1. Fill in the table as described on the next page.

Number of Games Needed to Win the Tournament	Winner	Tally of Tournaments Won	Total Tournaments Won
3	Team 1		
	Team 2		
4	Team 1		
	Team 2		
5	Team 1		
	Team 2		
	Total		25

Using Random Numbers (cont.)

2. Use coin tosses to play a "best-of-5" tournament. Make a tally mark in the Tally of Tournaments Won column of the table on page 260. The tally mark shows which team won the tournament and in how many games.

3. Play exactly 24 more tournaments. Make a tally mark to record the result for each tournament. Then convert the tally marks into numbers in the Total Tournaments Won column.

4. Use the table on page 260 to estimate the chance that a tournament takes

   a. exactly 3 games. _____%   b. exactly 4 games. _____%

   c. exactly 5 games. _____%   d. fewer than 5 games. _____%

Discuss the following situations with a partner. Record your ideas.

5. Suppose that there is a list of jobs that need to be done for your class (such as distributing supplies, collecting books, and taking messages to the office). How might you use random numbers to assign the jobs "at random," without using any pattern or showing favoritism?

   _____

   _____

   _____

   _____

6. You want to play a game. The rules are, "Roll 2 dice and add the numbers. Move your marker ahead that many spaces." You do not have any dice. How can you use number cards to play the game?

   _____

   _____

   _____

   _____

Mixed Practice

1. $(-49) + 52 =$ _____

2. $100 - (-35) =$ _____

3. $7 * (-90) =$ _____

4. $(-2{,}000) - 300 =$ _____

5. $(-40) * (-500) =$ _____

6. $2{,}100 \div (-3) =$ _____

7. $\frac{1}{2} * \frac{1}{2} =$ _____

8. $\frac{3}{4} + \frac{1}{2} =$ _____

9. $4 - \frac{3}{4} =$ _____

10. $\frac{1}{2}$ of $24 =$ _____

11. $\$1.25 + \$3.45 =$ _____

12. $1\frac{1}{2} + \left(-\frac{3}{4}\right) =$ _____

13. There are 11 classes at Washington School. Each class has about 28 students. What is a good estimate of the number of students at Washington School?

    About _____

                     (unit)

14. Stacy has saved $100.37. The picture frame she wants to buy for her parents' anniversary present is $47.56. Does she have enough money to buy two frames?

    _____

    Explain how you know. _____

    _____

    _____

Use with Lesson 7.3.

Math Boxes 7.3

1. Solve.

Solution

a. $\frac{n}{6} = 4$ _____

b. $\frac{42}{b} = 6$ _____

c. $\frac{5}{8} = \frac{t}{32}$ _____

d. $\frac{d}{18} = \frac{4}{6}$ _____

2. Fill in the missing equivalents.

Fraction	Decimal	Percent
$\frac{18}{20}$		
	0.98	
		60%
$\frac{7}{25}$		
		12.5%

3. The formula $C = (F - 32) * \frac{5}{9}$ can be used to convert temperatures from Fahrenheit to Celsius.

C is the temperature in degrees Celsius, and F is the temperature in degrees Fahrenheit. Calculate the temperature in degrees Celsius for the following Fahrenheit temperatures:

a. 68°F = _____°C

b. 41°F = _____°C

c. 131°F = _____°C

4. Multiply.

a.   602
   * 59
   _____

b.   218
   * 193
   _____

5. Write each number in standard notation.

a. 14.05 billion = _____

b. 2.3 trillion = _____

c. 389.1 million = _____

d. 5.07 billion = _____

e. 88.08 trillion = _____

6. Draw a triangle that has three acute angles.

Mazes and Tree Diagrams

The diagram at the right shows a maze. A person walking through the maze does not know in advance how many paths there are or how they divide.

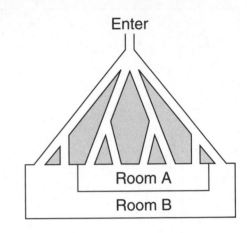

Enter

Room A

Room B

Pretend that you are walking through the maze. Each time the path divides, you select your next path at random. The paths that you can take next all have the same chance of being selected. You may not retrace your steps.

Depending on which paths you follow, you will end up in either Room A or Room B.

1. In which room are you more likely to end up—Room A or Room B? _____

2. Suppose 80 people took turns walking through the maze.

   a. About how many people would you expect to end up in Room A? _____

   b. About how many people would you expect to end up in Room B? _____

Your teacher will show you how to complete the following tree diagram. Or you can find out for yourself by reading pages 143 and 144 in the *Student Reference Book.*

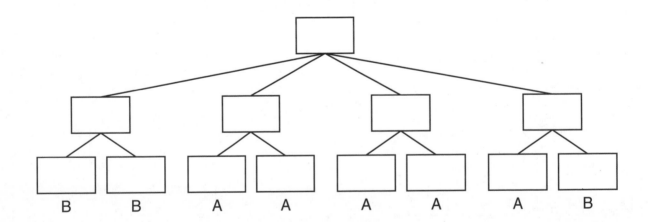

B   B   A   A   A   A   A   B

Maze Problems

1. Use the tree diagram below to help you solve the following problem.
   Suppose that 60 people walk through the maze below.

   a. About how many people would you expect to end up in Room A? _____

   b. About how many people would you expect to end up in Room B? _____

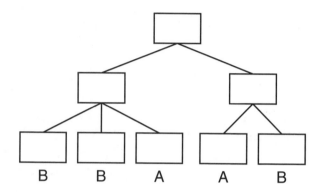

B   B   A   A   B

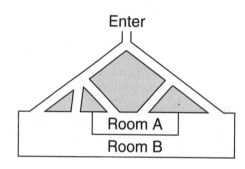

2. Make your own tree diagram to help you solve the following problem.
   Suppose that 120 people walk through the maze below.

   a. About how many people would you expect to end up in Room A? _____

   b. About how many people would you expect to end up in Room B? _____

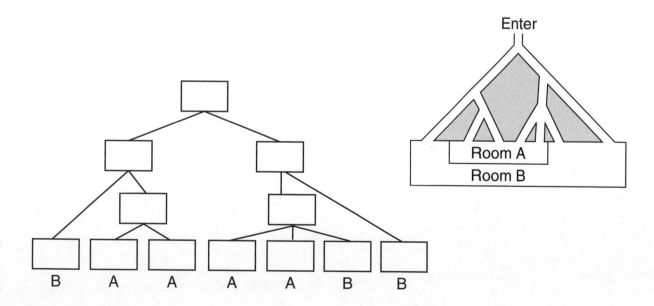

B   A   A   A   A   B   B

Math Boxes 7.4

1. Divide.

   a. 7)2,045

   b. 46)552

   c. 32)2,714

2. Complete the table
   for the formula below.
   Then plot the points
   to make a graph.

   Formula: 4h = g

h	g
1	
2	
3	
	20
	26

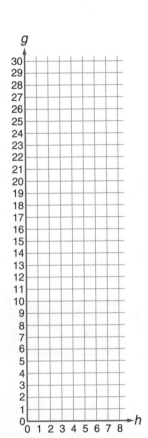

3. The highest point in North America is
   the top of Mt. McKinley, Alaska, with an
   elevation of 20,320 feet. The highest point
   in the lower 48 states of the United States
   is the top of Mt. Whitney, California, with
   an elevation of 14,494 feet. The lowest
   point in the United States is in Death
   Valley, California, at 282 feet below
   sea level.

   a. How much higher is the top of
      Mt. McKinley than Mt. Whitney?

      _____

   b. How many feet below Mt. McKinley
      is Death Valley?

      _____

Math Boxes 7.5

---

1. Multiply. Write each answer in simplest form.

a. _____ $= 3\frac{2}{3} * 2\frac{7}{8}$

b. _____ $= \frac{12}{10} * \frac{11}{5}$

c. _____ $= \frac{4}{3} * 3\frac{6}{7}$

d. $6\frac{1}{4} * 3\frac{11}{8} =$ _____

SRB
84–86

---

2. Solve the equation.

$7b + 16 = 5b + 24$

Solution _____

SRB
233

3. Add or subtract.

a. $23 + (-32) =$ _____

b. $-14 + (-78) =$ _____

c. _____ $= -800 + 275$

d. _____ $= 45 - 155$

e. _____ $= -195 - (-223)$

SRB
92 93

---

4. Complete.

a. $\frac{1}{10}$ of 268 = _____

b. $\frac{1}{100}$ of 21,509 = _____

c. $\frac{1}{1,000}$ of 7,834 = _____

d. $\frac{1}{100}$ of 72 = _____

SRB
48 49
83

5. Write the prime factorization for each number.

a. 36 = _____

b. 64 = _____

c. 58 = _____

d. 79 = _____

SRB
12

Use with Lesson 7.5.

267

Probability Tree Diagrams

Complete the tree diagram for each maze.

Write a fraction next to each branch to show the probability of selecting that branch. Then calculate the probability of reaching each endpoint. Record your answers in the blank spaces beneath the endpoints.

1. What is the probability of entering Room A? _____

   What is the probability of entering Room B? _____

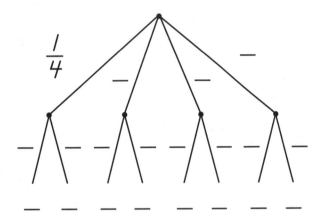

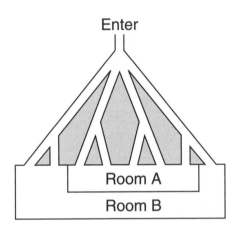

2. What is the probability of entering Room A? _____

   What is the probability of entering Room B? _____

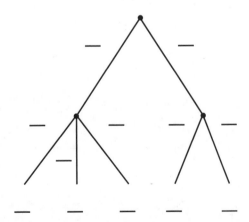

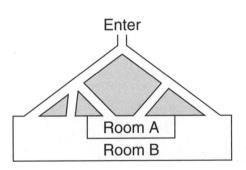

Use with Lesson 7.5.

Probability Tree Diagrams (cont.)

3. Josh has 3 clean shirts (red, blue, and green) and 2 clean pairs of pants (tan and black). He randomly selects one shirt. Then he randomly selects a pair of pants.

a. Complete the tree diagram. Write a fraction next to each branch to show the probability of selecting that branch.

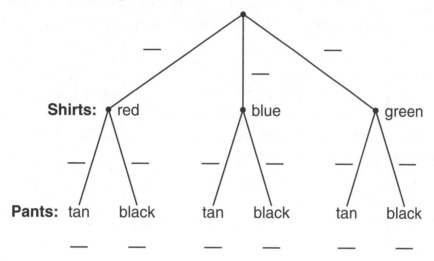

b. List all possible shirt-pants combinations. One has been done for you.

red–tan _____

_____

c. How many different shirt-pants combinations are there? _____

d. Do all of the shirt-pants combinations have the same chance of being selected?

_____

e. What is the probability that Josh will select

the blue shirt? _____   the blue shirt and the tan pants? _____

the tan pants? _____   a shirt that is not red? _____

the black pants and a shirt that is not red? _____

Venn Diagrams

A Venn diagram is a picture in which circles show relationships between sets.

Example 1

At Lincoln Middle School, every student is required to take a music class. 75 students play an instrument. They take a band or orchestra class. The remaining 300 students take a general music class. Students who take a band or orchestra class do not take the general music class.

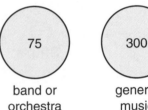

A Venn diagram illustrates this situation. The circles are drawn so that they do not overlap. This is because students who take a band or orchestra class do not take a general music class, and students who take a general music class do not take a band or orchestra class.

1. How many students are there at Lincoln Middle School? _____

Example 2

Ms. Barrie teaches both math and science. There are 26 students in her math class. There are 24 students in her science class. 5 of the students in her science class are also in her math class.

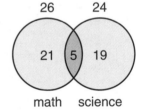

A Venn diagram of this situation shows overlapping circles. The overlapping part of the diagram represents the students who are in both Ms. Barrie's math class and her science class.

2. Ms. Barrie made a list of all of the students in her math and science classes. How many different names are on her list? _____

3. Write a number story for the Venn diagram at the right.

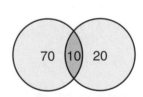

_____

_____

_____

_____

_____

More about Venn Diagrams

1. The sixth graders at Lincoln Middle School were asked whether they write with their left hands or right hands. A small number of students reported that they write equally well with either hand.

The survey results are shown in the Venn diagram at the right.

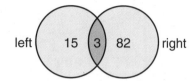

left (15 (3) 82) right

a. How many students were surveyed? _____ students

b. How many are *ambidextrous* (can write with either hand)? _____ students

c. How many always write with their left hands? _____ students

d. How many always write with their right hands? _____ students

e. How many never write with their left hands? _____ students

2. Mr. Carlson has 30 students in his sixth grade homeroom. After receiving their final test scores, he identified all students who scored 90% or above on each test. Mr. Carlson then drew this Venn diagram.

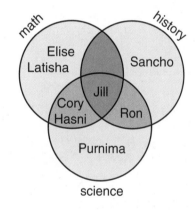

a. Whose performance was best overall? _____

b. Who scored 90% or above on *at least 2* tests? _____

c. Who scored 90% or above on *exactly 1* test? _____

d. Who scored 90% or above in both math and science? _____

e. Which two tests had the least overlap? _____

f. What percent of the students in Mr. Carlson's homeroom had a score of 90% or above on *exactly 2* tests? _____

Probability Tree Diagrams

Mr. Gulliver travels to and from work by train. Trains to work leave at 6, 7, 8, 9, and 10 A.M. Trains from work leave at 3, 4, and 5 P.M. Suppose Mr. Gulliver selects a morning train at random and then selects an afternoon train at random.

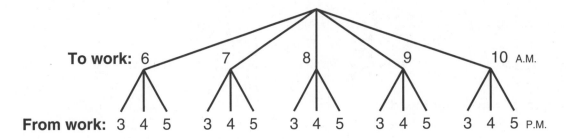

To work: 6   7   8   9   10 A.M.

From work: 3 4 5   3 4 5   3 4 5   3 4 5   3 4 5 P.M.

1. How many different combinations of trains to and from work can Mr. Gulliver take?

_____

Calculate the probability of each of the following.

2. Mr. Gulliver takes the 7 A.M. train to work.   _____

3. He returns home on the 4 P.M. train.   _____

4. He takes the 7 A.M. train to work and returns on the 4 P.M. train.   _____

5. He leaves for work on the 9 A.M. train and returns home on the 5 P.M. train.   _____

6. He leaves for work *before* 9 A.M.   _____

7. He leaves for work at 6 A.M. or 7 A.M. and returns home at 3 P.M.   _____

8. He returns home, but not on the 5 P.M. train.   _____

9. He boards the return train 9 hours after leaving for work.   _____

Math Boxes 7.6

---

1. Complete.

   a. 25% of 32 = _____

   b. 60% of 25 = _____

   c. _____ = 50% of 31

   d. _____ = $66\frac{2}{3}$% of 36

   e. _____ = 70% of 400

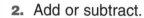
SRB
57

---

2. Add or subtract.

   a. 42.8 + 5.2 = _____

   b. 1.206 + 0.58 = _____

   c. $3.85 − $1.17 = _____

   d. _____ = 105.33 − 97.5

   e. _____ = 13.659 − 3.67

SRB
40 41

---

3. Fill in the missing numbers.

   a. 947 * 23 * 16 = 16 * 23 * _____

   b. 18 * 7 * 3 = 21 * _____

   c. _____ * 51 * 97 = 51 * 97 * 82

   d. _____ * 14 * 182 = 28 * 182

   e. _____ * 29 * 30 = 150 * 29

SRB
102

---

4. Write a number story for 5,893 / 15. Then solve the problem.

_____

_____

_____

Solution _____

SRB
242

---

5. For each of the following, tell which measure is needed: *perimeter, circumference, area,* or *volume.*

   a. Jean is going to tile her kitchen floor. She needs to know how many square-foot tiles to buy. _____

   b. Tyrone needs to add 1 drop of anti-chlorine solution to his aquarium for every 2 liters of water. He wants to know how many drops to add. _____

   c. Mrs. Vui plans to build a circular fence around her garden. She wants to know how much fencing to buy. _____

SRB
194–196
201

Fair and Unfair Games

A game of chance for two or more players is a **fair game** if each player has the same chance of winning. A game for one player is fair if the player has an equal chance of winning or losing. Any other game is an **unfair game.**

Each of the four games described below is for one player. Play Games 1, 2, and 3 a total of 6 times each. Tally the results. Later, the class will combine results for each game.

Game 1 Put 2 black counters and 1 white counter into a paper bag and shake the bag. Without looking, draw one counter. Then draw a second counter without putting the first counter back into the bag. If the 2 counters are the same color, you win. Otherwise, you lose. Play 6 games, and tally your results.

Tally for 6 games: Win _____   Lose _____

Do you think the game is fair?   _____

Combined class data: Win _____   Lose _____

Game 2 Use 2 black counters and 2 white counters. The rules are the same.

Tally for 6 games: Win _____   Lose _____

Do you think the game is fair?   _____

Combined class data: Win _____   Lose _____

Game 3 Use 3 black counters and 1 white counter. The rules are the same.

Tally for 6 games: Win _____   Lose _____

Do you think the game is fair?   _____

Combined class data: Win _____   Lose _____

Game 4 Suppose you use 4 black counters. The rules are the same.

Do you think the game is fair? _____

Explain your answer. _____

_____

_____

_____

Fair Games and Probability

You can use a tree diagram to decide whether a game is fair or unfair. This tree diagram represents Game 1 on page 274.

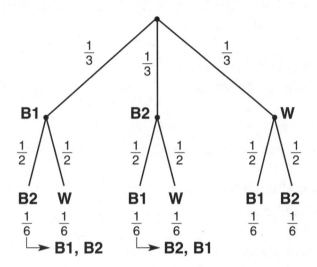

Before you draw the first counter, there are 3 counters in the bag. Although the 2 black counters look alike, they are not the same. To tell them apart, they are labeled B1 and B2. The probability of drawing either B1, B2, or W is $\frac{1}{3}$.

After the first draw, there are 2 counters left in the bag. The probability of drawing either of the 2 remaining counters is $\frac{1}{2}$.

There are 6 possible ways to draw the 2 remaining counters. The probability of each outcome is $\frac{1}{3} * \frac{1}{2}$, or $\frac{1}{6}$. There are 2 ways to draw the same color counters:

Draw B1 on the first draw and B2 on the second draw.
Draw B2 on the first draw and B1 on the second draw.

The chance of drawing 2 black counters is $\frac{1}{6} + \frac{1}{6}$, which is $\frac{2}{6}$, or $\frac{1}{3}$. Therefore, Game 1 is not a fair game.

Make tree diagrams to help you answer these questions.

1. What is the probability of winning Game 2? _____

2. Is Game 2 a fair game? _____

3. What is the probability of winning Game 3? _____

4. Is Game 3 a fair game? _____

Algebraic Expressions

1. Write an algebraic expression for each situation. Use the suggested variable.

   a. Jessica is 14 inches taller than Gerry. If Gerry is
      H inches tall, how many inches tall is Jessica?   _____ inches

   b. Sam ran for $\frac{4}{5}$ the length of time that Justin ran.
      If Justin ran R minutes, how long did Sam run?   _____ minutes

   c. Mary has X CDs in her collection. If Ann has 9 fewer
      CDs than Mary, how many CDs does Ann have?   _____ CDs

   d. Charlie has d dollars. Leanna has 6 times as much money
      as Charlie. How much money does Leanna have?   _____ dollars

   e. Erica has been a lifeguard for y years. That is 3 times as
      many years as Tom. How long has Tom been a lifeguard?   _____ years

2. Write the rule for the numbers in the table.

x	y
1.5	6.75
2	9
-3	-13.5
0.25	1.125

   Rule _____

3. Write the rule for the numbers in the table.

a	b
$\frac{2}{3}$	$\frac{4}{15}$
$\frac{1}{6}$	$\frac{1}{15}$
$\frac{3}{4}$	$\frac{3}{10}$
$\frac{4}{5}$	$\frac{8}{25}$

   Rule _____

First translate each situation from words into an algebraic expression.
Then solve the problem that follows.

4. Claire has 7 more crayons than 3 times the number of crayons Royce has.
   If Royce has C crayons, how many does Claire have?

   _____

   If Royce has 12 crayons, how many does Claire have? _____
                                                                           (unit)

5. Alinda has seen 4 fewer than $\frac{1}{2}$ the number of movies that her sister has seen.
   If her sister has seen M movies, how many has Alinda seen?

   _____

   If her sister has seen 20 movies, how many has Alinda seen? _____
                                                                                  (unit)

Use with Lesson 7.7.

Math Boxes 7.7

---

1. Multiply. Write each answer in simplest form.

a. $\dfrac{9}{5} * \dfrac{4}{3} =$ _____

b. _____ $= 1\dfrac{3}{8} * \dfrac{3}{4}$

c. _____ $= 2 * \dfrac{6}{7}$

d. $\dfrac{12}{4} * \dfrac{5}{3} =$ _____

---

2. Solve the equation.

$38 + y = 12 + 2y$

Solution _____

---

3. Add or subtract.

a. $55 + (-78) =$ _____

b. $94 - (-23) =$ _____

c. _____ $= -36 - (-65)$

d. _____ $= -18 - 27$

e. _____ $= -138 + 89$

---

4. Complete.

a. $\dfrac{709}{10} =$ _____

b. $\dfrac{83,261}{1,000} =$ _____

c. $\dfrac{352}{100} =$ _____

d. $\dfrac{96}{100} =$ _____

e. $\dfrac{247.8}{100} =$ _____

---

5. Write the prime factorization for each number.

a. $27 =$ _____

b. $45 =$ _____

c. $93 =$ _____

d. $57 =$ _____

Math Boxes 7.8

---

1. Complete.

   a. 75% of 44 = _____

   b. 80% of 70 = _____

   c. _____ = 37.5% of 32

   d. _____ = 90% of 36

   e. _____ = $33\frac{1}{3}$% of 1,200

---

2. Add or subtract.

   a. 26.25 + 16.31 = _____

   b. 635.2 − 55.89 = _____

   c. 2.043 − 0.8 = _____

   d. _____ = 0.97 − 0.404

   e. _____ = $106.39 + $68.28

---

3. Fill in the missing numbers.

   a. 58 * 91 * 27 = 27 * 58 * _____

   b. 24 * 16 * 10 = 240 * _____

   c. _____ * 35 * 94 = 35 * 94 * 87

   d. _____ * 500 = 25 * 20 * 153

   e. _____ * 426 * 81 = 81 * 945 * 426

---

4. Write a number story for $87\overline{)5,224}$.
Then solve the problem.

_____

_____

_____

Solution _____

---

5. For each of the following, tell which measure is needed:
perimeter, circumference, area, or *volume.*

   a. Warren plans to install wood molding where his
living room walls meet the ceiling. He needs to
know how much wood to buy.   _____

   b. Tina runs on a circular track. She knows the diameter
of the track. She wants to find the distance around.   _____

   c. Fertilizer is to be added to Flo's garden at the rate
of 1 cup for every 20 square feet. Flo wants to know
how much fertilizer to add.   _____

Narrowing Your Choices on Multiple-Choice Tests

Imagine that you are taking a multiple-choice test. Four possible answers are given for each question. You are to circle the correct answer. Suppose there are 20 questions for which you don't know the correct answer. You decide to guess for each of these questions.

1. What is the probability (chance) of answering a question correctly? _____

2. How many of the 20 questions would you expect to answer correctly by guessing? _____

Explain. _____

_____

3. In scoring the test, each correct answer is worth 1 point. To discourage guessing, there is a penalty of $\frac{1}{3}$ point for each incorrect answer. Do you think this is a fair penalty for an incorrect answer? _____

Explain. _____

_____

_____

_____

When you play board games or card games or answer fun quizzes in which there is no penalty for guessing incorrectly, guessing can be a valuable tool for improving your score. You can improve your chances of guessing correctly, if you are able to eliminate some of the choices before you guess. On the following pages, you will investigate the advantages (or disadvantages) that can result from guessing on multiple-choice tests.

Guessing is usually not encouraged for school tests or achievement tests, even if a penalty is not imposed for incorrect answers. A score that is inflated by guessing gives a misleading view of the test taker's skills and knowledge.

Guessing on Multiple-Choice Tests

1. For each question on the following test, first draw a line through each answer that you know is not correct. Then circle one answer for each question. If you do not know the correct answer, guess.

Number correct _____

---

1. A nautical mile is equal to

   a. 1 foot.

   b. 1 yard.

   c. 1,832 meters.

   d. 1,852 meters.

2. In 1994, the population of Nevada was

   a. 1 billion.

   b. 1,475,028.

   c. 1,457,028.

   d. 14,628.

3. Which region receives the greatest average annual rainfall?

   a. Atlanta, Georgia

   b. New Orleans, Louisiana

   c. Mojave Desert, California

   d. Sahara Desert, Africa

4. The addition sign (+) was introduced into mathematics by

   a. Johann Widman.

   b. Johann Rahn.

   c. Abraham Lincoln.

   d. Martin Luther King, Jr.

5. How many diagonals does a 13-sided polygon (13-gon) have?

   a. 1

   b. 54

   c. 65

   d. 13,000

6. The leading cause of death in the United States is

   a. bungee jumping.

   b. cancer.

   c. drowning.

   d. heart disease.

Use with Lesson 7.8.

Guessing on Multiple-Choice Tests (cont.)

2. When you can narrow the choices for a question to two possible answers, what is the chance of guessing the correct answer? _____

3. How many of the 6 questions on page 280 do you think you answered correctly?

   _____ questions

4. Is it likely that you got all 6 correct? _____

5. Is it likely that you got all 6 wrong? _____

6. Suppose each correct answer is worth 1 point and each incorrect answer carries a penalty of $\frac{1}{3}$ point. Complete the Total Points column of the table. You will complete the Class Tally column later.

Number Correct	Number Incorrect	Total Points	Class Tally
6	0	6	
5	1		
4	2		
3	3		
2	4	$2 - \frac{4}{3} = \frac{2}{3}$	
1	5		
0	6		

Guessing on Multiple-Choice Tests (cont.)

7. For each question on the following test, first draw a line through each answer that you know is not correct. Then circle one answer for each question. If you do not know the correct answer, guess.

Number correct _____

---

1. The neck of a 152-pound person weighs about

   a. 100 pounds.

   b. $12\frac{1}{2}$ pounds.

   c. $11\frac{1}{2}$ pounds.

   d. $10\frac{1}{2}$ pounds.

2. The average height of a full grown weeping willow tree is

   a. 50 feet.

   b. 45 feet.

   c. 35 feet.

   d. 2 feet.

3. The normal daily high temperature for July in Cleveland, Ohio, is

   a. 84°F.

   b. 82°F.

   c. 80°F.

   d. 0°F.

4. The circumference of Earth at the equator is about

   a. 24,901.6 miles.

   b. 24,801.6 miles.

   c. 24,701.6 miles.

   d. 2,000 miles.

5. In 1994, the average American consumed about 141 pounds of which food?

   a. sugar

   b. spinach

   c. potatoes

   d. rice

6. A slice of white bread has about how many calories?

   a. 3

   b. 65

   c. 70

   d. 75

Use with Lesson 7.8.

Guessing on Multiple-Choice Tests (cont.)

8. When you can narrow the choices for a question to three possible answers, what is the chance of guessing the correct answer? _____

9. How many of the six questions do you think you answered correctly?

_____ questions

10. Is it likely that you got all six correct? _____

11. Is it likely that you got all six wrong? _____

12. Suppose each correct answer is worth 1 point and each incorrect answer carries a penalty of $\frac{1}{3}$ point. Complete the Total Points column of the table below.

Number Correct	Number Incorrect	Total Points	Class Tally
6	0	6	
5	1		
4	2		
3	3		
2	4	$2 - \frac{4}{3} = \frac{2}{3}$	
1	5		
0	6		

Time to Reflect

1. In this unit, you have been studying probability. Describe at least one way in which probability is part of your daily life.

_____

_____

_____

_____

_____

2. How would you describe a fair game to someone who didn't know what it was?

_____

_____

_____

_____

_____

3. Explain how drawing a probability tree diagram might help you solve a problem.

_____

_____

_____

_____

_____

4. Explain how you can get a better score on a multiple-choice test even if you don't know all of the answers.

_____

_____

_____

_____

_____

Math Boxes 7.9

1. Divide.

    a. $34\overline{)826}$ **b.** $75\overline{)7,698}$ **c.** $53\overline{)2,005}$

2. Complete.

    a. 20% of 80 = _____

    b. 75% of 48 = _____

    c. 55% of 1,000 = _____

    d. 30% of 250 = _____

    e. 80% of 70 = _____

3. Solve.

                         Solution

    a. $\frac{28}{c} = 14$ _____

    b. $\frac{25}{75} = \frac{d}{12}$ _____

    c. $\frac{15}{33} = \frac{5}{x}$ _____

    d. $\frac{m}{21} = \frac{5}{7}$ _____

    e. $\frac{500}{10,000} = \frac{p}{100}$ _____

4. Multiply. Write your answer in simplest form.

    a. $\frac{1}{2} * 5\frac{3}{4} =$ _____   **b.** _____ $= 3 * \frac{5}{8}$ **c.** _____ $= 2\frac{1}{5} * \frac{3}{22}$

    d. _____ $= \frac{14}{6} * \frac{8}{7}$ **e.** $\frac{20}{100} * \frac{18}{8} =$ _____   **f.** $4\frac{3}{4} * \frac{3}{4} =$ _____

Solving Rate Problems

Math Message

1. A computer printer prints 6 pages in 2 minutes.
   How many pages will it print in 5 minutes?   _____

2. Jessica trains at an indoor track during the winter.
   She can run 24 laps in 8 minutes. At this rate, how
   many laps can Jessica run in 12 minutes?   _____

3. Ms. Marquez is reading stories her students wrote.
   She has read 5 stories in 40 minutes.

   a. At this rate, how long would it take her to read 1 story?   _____

   b. How long will it take her to read all 30 of her students' stories?   _____

   c. Complete the proportion to show your solution.

   $$\frac{5 \text{ stories}}{40 \text{ minutes}} = \frac{30 \text{ stories}}{\boxed{} \text{ minutes}}$$

4. Sam scored 75 points in the first 5 basketball games.

   a. On average, how many points did he score per game?   _____

   b. At this rate, how many points might he score in a 15-game season?   _____

   c. Complete the proportion to show your solution.

   $$\frac{75 \text{ points}}{5 \text{ games}} = \frac{\boxed{} \text{ points}}{15 \text{ games}}$$

5. Last year, 55 students sold $1,210 worth of candy for their band's fund-raiser.

   a. On average, how many dollars' worth of candy did each student sell? _____

   b. This year, 67 students will be selling candy. If they sell at the
      same rate as last year, how much money can they expect to raise?   _____

   c. Complete the proportion to show your solution.

   $$\frac{\boxed{} \text{ students}}{\$ \boxed{}} = \frac{\boxed{} \text{ students}}{\$ \boxed{}}$$

6. Art worked at the checkout counter from 5:30 P.M. to 11 P.M. He earned $33.

   a. How much did he earn per hour?   _____

   b. Art works $27\frac{1}{2}$ hours per week. How much will he earn in 1 week?   _____

   c. Complete the proportion to show your solution.

   $$\frac{\$ \boxed{}}{\boxed{} \text{ hours}} = \frac{\$ \boxed{}}{\boxed{} \text{ hours}}$$

Use with Lesson 8.1.

Solving Rate Problems (cont.)

7. The furlong is a unit of distance. This unit is now most commonly used in horse racing. There are 40 furlongs in 5 miles.

   a. Fill in the rate table.

miles	1	2		5	8	10
furlongs			24	40		

   b. How many furlongs are there in 8 miles? _____

   Complete the proportion to show your solution.

   $$\frac{\boxed{} \text{ miles}}{\boxed{} \text{ furlongs}} = \frac{\boxed{} \text{ miles}}{\boxed{} \text{ furlongs}}$$

   c. How many miles are there in 8 furlongs? _____

   Complete the proportion to show your solution.

   $$\frac{\boxed{} \text{ miles}}{\boxed{} \text{ furlongs}} = \frac{\boxed{} \text{ miles}}{\boxed{} \text{ furlongs}}$$

8. Nico read a 240-page book in 6 hours.

   a. Fill in the rate table.

pages		120		240	80	
hours	1		4	6		8

   b. At this rate, how long would it take him to read a 160-page book? _____

   Complete the proportion to show your solution.

   $$\frac{\boxed{} \text{ pages}}{\boxed{} \text{ hours}} = \frac{\boxed{} \text{ pages}}{\boxed{} \text{ hours}}$$

   c. How many hours did it take him to read 80 pages? _____

   Complete the proportion to show your solution.

   $$\frac{\boxed{} \text{ pages}}{\boxed{} \text{ hours}} = \frac{\boxed{} \text{ pages}}{\boxed{} \text{ hours}}$$

Use any method you wish to solve the following problems. Write a proportion to show your solution.

9. A recipe for a 2-pound loaf of bread calls for 4 cups of flour. How many 2-pound loaves can you make with 12 cups of flour? _____

   $$\frac{\boxed{} \text{ loaves}}{\boxed{} \text{ cups}} = \frac{\boxed{} \text{ loaves}}{\boxed{} \text{ cups}}$$

10. Two inches of rain fell between 7 A.M. and 3 P.M. It continued to rain at the same rate until 7 P.M.

    How many inches of rain fell between 7 A.M. and 7 P.M.? _____

    $$\frac{\boxed{} \text{ inches}}{\boxed{} \text{ hours}} = \frac{\boxed{} \text{ inches}}{\boxed{} \text{ hours}}$$

Use with Lesson 8.1.

Division Practice

Divide. Show your work in the space below.
In Problems 1–3, write your answer as a mixed number.

1. 5,875 ÷ 34 = _____

2. 958 / 18 = _____

3. 2,509 / 64 = _____

In Problems 4–6, round your answer to the nearest whole number.

4. 38,419 ÷ 57 = _____

5. 7,648 ÷ 84 = _____

6. 10,063 / 23 = _____

7. Write a number story for Problem 6.

_____

_____

_____

_____

_____

_____

Use with Lesson 8.1.

Math Boxes 8.1

1. Circle the number sentences that are true.

   a. $(18 + 9) \div 3 + 6 = 15$

   b. $32 \div 8 * 4^2 = 1$

   c. $30 = 90 \div 10 + 20$

   d. $1 = 100 - 75 / 5^2$

   e. $14 - (7 * 2) + 6 = 6$

2. Insert the decimal point in the product.

   a. $4.02 * 85 =$ 3 4 1 7

   b. $-9.6 * 38.82 =$ −3 7 2 6 7 2

   c. $67 * 1.004 =$ 6 7 2 6 8

   d. $0.89 * -5.1 =$ −4 5 3 9

   e. $-2.307 * -1.9 =$ 4 3 8 3 3

3. Without using a protractor, find the measure in degrees of each numbered angle. Write each measure on the drawing. (Lines *a* and *b* are parallel.)

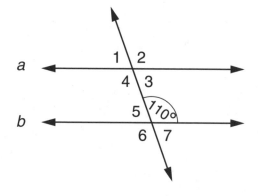

4. Fill in the blanks. (*Hint:* For decimals, think fractions.)

   a. $\frac{4}{9} *$ _____ $= 1$

   b. $\frac{11}{12} *$ _____ $= 1$

   c. $\frac{16}{5} *$ _____ $= 1$

   d. $0.3 *$ _____ $= 1$

   e. $0.06 *$ _____ $= 1$

5. Molly filled a measuring cup with milk to the $\frac{3}{4}$-cup mark. Now she wants to add $\frac{1}{2}$ cup of buttermilk to the cup. To what mark should she pour the buttermilk?

_____
            (unit)

Rate Problems and Proportions

Math Message

Solve the problems below. Then write a proportion for each problem.

1. Robin rode her bike at an average speed of 8 miles per hour.
   At this rate, how far would she travel in 3 hours?   _____

   $$\frac{\boxed{}\ \text{miles}}{\boxed{}\ \text{hours}} = \frac{\boxed{}\ \text{miles}}{\boxed{}\ \text{hours}}$$

2. A high-speed copier makes 90 copies per minute.
   How long will it take to make 270 copies?   _____

   $$\frac{\boxed{}\ \text{copies}}{\boxed{}\ \text{minutes}} = \frac{\boxed{}\ \text{copies}}{\boxed{}\ \text{minutes}}$$

3. Talia rode her bike at an average speed of 10 miles per hour.
   At this rate, how long would it take Talia to ride 15 miles?   _____

   $$\frac{\boxed{}\ \text{miles}}{\boxed{}\ \text{hours}} = \frac{\boxed{}\ \text{miles}}{\boxed{}\ \text{hours}}$$

For each of the following problems, first complete the rate table. Use the table to write an open proportion. Solve the proportion. Then write the answer to the problem. Study the first problem.

4. Angela earns $6 per hour baby-sitting. How long must she work to earn $72?

dollars	6	72
hours	1	t

   $$\overset{*\ 12}{\overbrace{}}$$
   $$\frac{\boxed{6}}{\boxed{1}} = \frac{\boxed{72}}{\boxed{t}}$$
   $$\underset{*\ 12}{\underbrace{}}$$

   Answer: Angela must work _____ hours to earn $72.

5. There are 9 calories per gram of fat. How many grams of fat are there in 63 calories?

calories		
grams (of fat)		

   $$\frac{\boxed{}}{\boxed{}} = \frac{\boxed{}}{\boxed{}}$$

   Answer: There are _____ grams of fat in 63 calories.

Rate Problems and Proportions (cont.)

6. If carpet costs $22.95 per square yard, how much will 12 square yards of carpet cost?

dollars		
square yards		

$$\frac{\quad}{\quad} = \frac{\quad}{\quad}$$

Answer: 12 square yards

of carpet will cost _____ .

7. There are 80 calories in 1 serving of soup. How many servings of soup contain 120 calories?

calories		
servings		

$$\frac{\quad}{\quad} = \frac{\quad}{\quad}$$

Answer: There are 120 calories

in _____ servings of soup.

8. A car goes 480 miles on a 12-gallon tank of gas. How many miles is this per gallon?

miles		
gallons		

$$\frac{\quad}{\quad} = \frac{\quad}{\quad}$$

Answer: The car will go _____ miles on one gallon of gas.

9. Arun read the first 48 pages of a mystery novel in 3 hours. At this rate, how long will it take him to read 80 pages?

hours		
pages		

$$\frac{\quad}{\quad} = \frac{\quad}{\quad}$$

Answer: It will take Arun _____ hours to read 80 pages.

10. A TV station runs 42 minutes of commercials in seven half-hour programs. How many minutes of commercials does it run per hour?

commercial minutes		
hours		

$$\frac{\quad}{\quad} = \frac{\quad}{\quad}$$

Answer: The station runs _____ minutes of commercials per hour.

More Division Practice

Divide. Show your work in the space below.
In Problems 1–3, write the answers as 1-place decimals.

1. $571 \div 8 =$ _____

2. $2{,}723 / 94 =$ _____

3. $815 \div 46 =$ _____

In Problems 4–6, write the answers as 2-place decimals.

4. $89 / 6 =$ _____

5. $3{,}714 / 42 =$ _____

6. $217 \div 18 =$ _____

7. Write a number story for Problem 6.

_____

_____

_____

_____

_____

_____

Use with Lesson 8.2.

Math Boxes 8.2

1. Solve the equation.

$$45 - 3g = g + 33$$

Solution _____

2. Complete.

a. $\frac{3}{4}$ of 280 = _____

b. $\frac{4}{12}$ of 303 = _____

c. $\frac{5}{6}$ of 420 = _____

d. $\frac{2}{9}$ of 360 = _____

e. $\frac{3}{5}$ of 1,200 = _____

3. Janine watches about 12 hours of television per week.
Complete the table. Then use your protractor to make
a circle graph of the information.

Type of Show	Number of Hours	Percent of Hours	Degrees
Comedy	4		
Educational	1		
News	2		
Sports	3		
Cartoon	2		
Total			

(title)

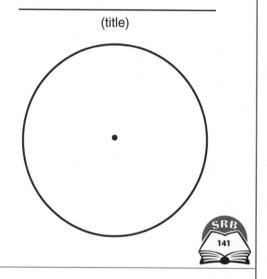

4. Solve.

Solution

a. $\frac{42}{18} = \frac{x}{3}$ _____

b. $\frac{125}{n} = \frac{5}{1}$ _____

c. $\frac{36}{w} = \frac{18}{2}$ _____

d. $\frac{d}{150} = \frac{3}{5}$ _____

e. $\frac{90}{3} = \frac{9}{u}$ _____

5. Divide. Show your work.

$$18\overline{)2{,}020}$$

Equivalent Fractions and Cross Products

For Part a of each problem, write = or ≠ in the answer box.
For Part b, calculate the cross products.

1. a. $\frac{3}{5}$ ☐ $\frac{6}{10}$

 b. $\frac{3}{5}$ ✕ $\frac{6}{10}$ 5 * 6 = _____

          3 * 10 = _____

2. a. $\frac{7}{8}$ ☐ $\frac{2}{3}$

 b. $\frac{7}{8}$ ✕ $\frac{2}{3}$ 8 * 2 = _____

          7 * 3 = _____

3. a. $\frac{2}{3}$ ☐ $\frac{6}{9}$

 b. $\frac{2}{3}$ ✕ $\frac{6}{9}$ 3 * 6 = _____

          2 * 9 = _____

4. a. $\frac{6}{9}$ ☐ $\frac{8}{12}$

 b. $\frac{6}{9}$ ✕ $\frac{8}{12}$ 9 * 8 = _____

          6 * 12 = _____

5. a. $\frac{2}{8}$ ☐ $\frac{4}{12}$

 b. $\frac{2}{8}$ ✕ $\frac{4}{12}$ 8 * 4 = _____

          2 * 12 = _____

6. a. $\frac{10}{12}$ ☐ $\frac{5}{8}$

 b. $\frac{10}{12}$ ✕ $\frac{5}{8}$ 12 * 5 = _____

          10 * 8 = _____

7. a. $\frac{1}{4}$ ☐ $\frac{5}{20}$

 b. $\frac{1}{4}$ ✕ $\frac{5}{20}$ 4 * 5 = _____

          1 * 20 = _____

8. a. $\frac{5}{7}$ ☐ $\frac{15}{21}$

 b. $\frac{5}{7}$ ✕ $\frac{15}{21}$ 7 * 15 = _____

          5 * 21 = _____

9. a. $\frac{10}{16}$ ☐ $\frac{4}{8}$

 b. $\frac{10}{16}$ ✕ $\frac{4}{8}$ 16 * 4 = _____

          10 * 8 = _____

10. a. $\frac{3}{5}$ ☐ $\frac{10}{15}$

 b. $\frac{3}{5}$ ✕ $\frac{10}{15}$ 5 * 10 = _____

          3 * 15 = _____

11. What pattern can you find in Parts a and b in the problems above?

_____

_____

_____

Math Boxes 8.3

---

1. Insert parentheses to make each number sentence true.

   a. $0.01 * 7 + 9 / 4 = 0.04$

   b. $\frac{4}{5} * 25 - 10 / 2 = 15$

   c. $\sqrt{64} / 5 + 3 * 3 = 3$

   d. $5 * 10^2 + 10^2 * 2 = 2{,}000$

   e. $5 * 10^2 + 10^2 * 2 = 700$

2. Insert the decimal point in the product.

   a. $3.6 * 5.35 = $ 1 9 2 6

   b. $-299 * -0.03 = $ 8 9 7

   c. $218 * 2.15 = $ 4 6 8 7

   d. $-6.56 * 3.03 = $ − 1 9 8 7 6 8

   e. $25 * -0.025 = $ − 6 2 5

---

3. Without using a protractor, find the measure in degrees of each numbered angle. Write each measure on the drawing. (Lines a and b are parallel.)

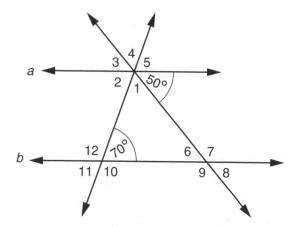

---

4. Fill in the blanks. (*Hint:* For decimals, think fractions.)

   a. $\frac{3}{5} * $ _____ $= 1$

   b. $\frac{8}{9} * $ _____ $= 1$

   c. $\frac{7}{3} * $ _____ $= 1$

   d. $0.01 * $ _____ $= 1$

   e. $0.5 * $ _____ $= 1$

5. Cherie made a deal with her mother. If Cherie could mow the lawn in 1 hour or less, she would get paid double. In 45 minutes, she mowed $\frac{7}{10}$ of the lawn. If she continues to mow at the same rate, will she finish mowing the lawn in time to be paid double?

   _____ Explain. _____

   _____

   _____

Solving Proportions with Cross Products

Use cross multiplication to solve these proportions.

Example $\dfrac{4}{6} = \dfrac{p}{15}$

$6 * p$

$4 * 15$

$6 * p = 4 * 15$

$6 * p = 60$

$p = 60 / 6 = 10$

1. $\dfrac{3}{6} = \dfrac{y}{10}$ _____

2. $\dfrac{7}{21} = \dfrac{3}{c}$ _____

3. $\dfrac{m}{20} = \dfrac{2}{8}$ _____

4. $\dfrac{2}{10} = \dfrac{5}{z}$ _____

5. $\dfrac{9}{15} = \dfrac{12}{k}$ _____

6. $\dfrac{10}{12} = \dfrac{d}{9}$ _____

For each problem on the next page, set up a proportion, solve the proportion with cross multiplication, and then write the answer.

Example Jessie swam 6 lengths of the pool in 4 minutes. At this rate, how many lengths will she swim in 10 minutes?

Proportion: $\dfrac{\boxed{6\ lengths}}{\boxed{4\ minutes}} = \dfrac{\boxed{n\ lengths}}{\boxed{10\ minutes}}$

Solution: $\dfrac{6}{4} \diagdown \dfrac{n}{10}$

$4 * n$

$6 * 10$

$4 * n = 6 * 10$

$4 * n = 60$

$n = 60 / 4 = 15$

Answer: Jessie will swim _____ lengths in 10 minutes.

Use with Lesson 8.3.

Solving Proportions with Cross Products (cont.)

7. Belle bought 8 yards of ribbon for $6. How many yards could she buy for $9?

Solution:

$$\frac{\boxed{}}{\boxed{}} = \frac{\boxed{}}{\boxed{}}$$

Answer: Belle could buy _____ yards of ribbon for $9.

8. Before going to France, Maurice exchanged $25 for 125 French francs. At that exchange rate, how many French francs could he get for $80?

Solution:

$$\frac{\boxed{}}{\boxed{}} = \frac{\boxed{}}{\boxed{}}$$

Answer: Maurice could get _____ French francs for $80.

9. One gloomy day, 4 inches of rain fell in 6 hours. At this rate, how many inches of rain had fallen after 4 hours?

Solution:

$$\frac{\boxed{}}{\boxed{}} = \frac{\boxed{}}{\boxed{}}$$

Answer: _____ inches of rain had fallen in 4 hours.

10. Ben's apartment building has 9 flights of stairs. To climb to the top floor, he must go up 144 steps. How many steps must he climb to get to the fifth floor?

Solution:

$$\frac{\boxed{}}{\boxed{}} = \frac{\boxed{}}{\boxed{}}$$

Answer: Ben must climb _____ steps.

11. At sea level, sound travels 0.62 mile in 3 seconds. What is the speed of sound in miles per hour? (*Hint:* First find the number of seconds in 1 hour.)

Solution:

$$\frac{\boxed{}}{\boxed{}} = \frac{\boxed{}}{\boxed{}}$$

Answer: Sound travels at the rate of _____ miles per hour.

Decimal Division Practice

First, estimate the answer. Write a number model for your estimate. Then divide, ignoring the decimal point. Use your estimate to help you decide where to place the decimal point in the answer.

1. 59.64 / 7

Estimate _____

Answer _____

2. 185.6 ÷ 29

Estimate _____

Answer _____

3. 733.6 ÷ 56

Estimate _____

Answer _____

4. 946.74 / 62

Estimate _____

Answer _____

5. 7,219.08 / 4

Estimate _____

Answer _____

6. 351.5 / 95

Estimate _____

Answer _____

Use with Lesson 8.3.

Rate * Time = Distance

For each problem, make a rate table. Then write a number model and solve it.
Write the answer.

1. Ms. Riley drove her car at 60 miles per hour
for 4 hours. How far did she travel?

Number model _____

Answer: She traveled _____
miles in 4 hours.

2. A bamboo plant grows 8 inches per day.
How tall will it be after 7 days?

Number model _____

Answer: The plant will be _____
inches tall.

3. A rocket is traveling at 40,000 miles per hour.
How far will it travel in 168 hours?

Number model _____

Answer: The rocket will travel _____
miles in 168 hours.

4. Chelsea can ride her bicycle at 9 miles
per hour. At this rate, how long will it take
her to ride 30 miles?

Number model _____

Answer: It will take her _____
hours to ride 30 miles.

5. Australia is moving about 3 inches per year
with respect to the southern Pacific Ocean.
How many *feet* will it move in 50 years?

Number model _____

Answer: Australia will move _____
feet in 50 years.

Use with Lesson 8.4.

How Many Calories Do You Use Per Day?

Your body needs food. It uses the materials in food to produce energy—energy to keep your body warm and moving, to live and grow, and to build and repair muscles and tissues.

The amount of energy a food will produce when it is digested by the body is measured in a unit called the **calorie.** A calorie is not a substance in food.

1. The following table shows the number of calories per minute and per hour used by the average sixth grader for various activities. Complete the table. Round your answers for calories per minute to the nearest tenth and calories per hour to the nearest ten.

Calorie Use by Average 6th Graders		
Activity	Calories/Minute	Calories/Hour
Sleeping	0.7	40
Studying, writing, sitting	1.2	70
Eating, talking, sitting in class	1.2	70
Standing	1.3	80
Dressing, undressing		90
Walking (slowly, at 2 mph)	2.2	130
Walking (briskly, at 3.5 mph)	3.0	180
Doing housework, gardening	2.0	
Vacuuming	2.7	160
Raking leaves	3.7	220
Shoveling snow	5.0	300
Bicycling (6 mph)		170
Bicycling (13 mph)	4.5	
Bicycling (20 mph)	8.3	
Running (5 mph)	6.0	360
Running (7.5 mph)		560
Swimming (20 yards/minute)	3.3	200
Swimming (40 yards/minute)	5.8	350
Basketball, soccer (vigorous)	9.7	580
Volleyball	4.0	240
Aerobic dancing (vigorous)	6.0	360
Square dancing	4.0	240

How Many Calories Do You Use Per Day? (cont.)

2. Think of all of the things you do during a typical 24-hour school day.

   a. List your activities in the table below.

   b. Record your estimate of the time you spend on each activity (to the nearest fifteen minutes). Be sure that the times add up to 24 hours.

   c. For each activity, record the number of calories used per minute or per hour. Then calculate the number of calories you use for the activity.

Example

Suppose you spend 8 hours and 15 minutes sleeping.
Choose the per-hour rate: Sleeping uses 40 calories per hour.
Multiply: 8.25 hours $*$ 40 calories per hour = 330 calories

My Activities During a Typical 24-Hour School Day			
Activity	Time Spent on Activity	Calorie Rate (cal/min or cal/hr)	Calories Used for Activity

3. When you have completed the table, find the total number of calories you use in a typical 24-hour day.

   In a typical 24-hour school day, I use about _____ calories.

Using Unit Fractions to Find a Whole

Example 1

Alex collects sports cards. Seventy of the cards feature basketball players. These 70 cards are $\frac{2}{3}$ of Alex's collection. How many sports cards does Alex have?

- If $\frac{2}{3}$ of the collection is 70 cards, then $\frac{1}{3}$ is 35 cards.
- Alex has all of the cards—that's $\frac{3}{3}$ of the cards.
- Therefore, Alex has 3 * 35, or 105 cards.

Example 2

Barb's mother baked cookies. She gave Barb 12 cookies, which were $\frac{2}{5}$ of the total number she baked. How many cookies did Barb's mother bake?

- If $\frac{2}{5}$ of the total is 12 cookies, then $\frac{1}{5}$ is 6 cookies.
- Barb's mother baked all the cookies—that's $\frac{5}{5}$ of the cookies.
- She baked 5 * 6, or 30 cookies.

1. Six jars are filled with cookies. The number of cookies in each jar is not known. For each clue given in the table, find the number of cookies in the jar.

Clue	Number of Cookies in Jar
$\frac{1}{2}$ jar contains 31 cookies.	
$\frac{2}{8}$ jar contains 10 cookies.	
$\frac{3}{5}$ jar contains 36 cookies.	
$\frac{3}{8}$ jar contains 21 cookies.	
$\frac{4}{7}$ jar contains 64 cookies.	
$\frac{3}{11}$ jar contains 45 cookies.	

2. Alan is walking to a friend's house. He has gone $\frac{6}{10}$ of the distance in 48 minutes. If he continues at the same speed, about how long will the entire walk take?

_____

3. A candle burned $\frac{3}{8}$ of the way down in 36 minutes. If it continues to burn at the same rate, about how many more minutes will the candle burn before it is used up?

_____

Use with Lesson 8.4.

Math Boxes 8.4

1. Solve the equation.

$(18 \div 2)C = 56 + C$

Solution _____

2. Complete.

a. $\frac{1}{3}$ of 216 = _____

b. $\frac{5}{8}$ of 160 = _____

c. $\frac{9}{10}$ of 300 = _____

d. $\frac{3}{20}$ of 420 = _____

e. $\frac{5}{7}$ of 777 = _____

3. Peabody's Bookstore had a sale. Complete the table.
Then use your protractor to make a circle graph
of the information.

Book Category	Number Sold	Percent of Total	Degrees
Fiction	280		
Sports	283		
Children's	125		
Travel	212		
Computer	100		
Total			

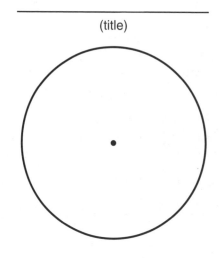

_____
(title)

4. Solve.

Solution

a. $\frac{3}{4} = \frac{m}{28}$ _____

b. $\frac{12}{16} = \frac{p}{32}$ _____

c. $\frac{14}{1} = \frac{42}{g}$ _____

d. $\frac{5}{14} = \frac{f}{28}$ _____

e. $\frac{250}{20} = \frac{2.5}{u}$ _____

5. Divide. Show your work.

$38\overline{)4{,}087}$

Food Nutrition Labels

Study the food label at the right for a container of low-fat yogurt.

- There are 240 calories per serving. There are 3 grams of fat per serving.

- There are 44 grams of carbohydrate per serving. The label does not indicate how many calories come from carbohydrate, but it does provide the information you need to calculate the number of calories from carbohydrate. One gram of carbohydrate generates 4 calories of energy. So 44 grams generates 44 grams * 4 calories per gram, or 176 calories.

- There are 9 grams of protein per serving. One gram of protein generates 4 calories. So 9 grams generates 9 grams * 4 calories per gram, or 36 calories.

Nutrition Facts
Serving Size 1 container (227 g)

Amount Per Serving

Calories 240 Calories from Fat 27

% Daily Value

Total Fat 3 g	**5%**
Saturated Fat 1.5 g	**8%**
Cholesterol 15 mg	**5%**
Sodium 150 mg	**6%**
Potassium 450 mg	**13%**
Total Carbohydrate 44 g	**15%**
Dietary Fiber 1 g	**4%**
Sugars 43 g	
Protein 9 g	

Vitamin A 2%   •   Vitamin C 10%
Calcium 35%   •   Iron 0%

Calories per gram:
Fat 9 • Carbohydrate 4 • Protein 4

For each food label below, record the number of calories from fat. Then calculate the numbers of calories from carbohydrate and from protein. Add to find the total calories per serving.

Nutrition Facts
Serving Size 1 slice (23 g)
Servings Per Container 20

Amount Per Serving

Calories 65   Calories from Fat 9

% Daily Value

Total Fat 1 g	2%
Total Carbohydrate 12 g	4%
Protein 2 g	

White bread

Nutrition Facts
Serving Size 1 link (45 g)
Servings Per Container 10

Amount Per Serving

Calories 150 Calories from Fat 120

% Daily Value

Total Fat 13 g	**20%**
Total Carbohydrate 1 g	<1%
Protein 7 g	

Hot dog

1. Calories

   From fat _____

   From carbohydrate _____

   From protein _____

   Total calories _____

2. Calories

   From fat _____

   From carbohydrate _____

   From protein _____

   Total calories _____

3. Does the total number of calories per serving shown on each food label agree with the total calories you calculated? _____

Use with Lesson 8.5.

Math Boxes 8.5

1. The area of Square *CAMP* is 25 cm². Squares *CAMP* and *MADE* are congruent. What is the area of Triangle *APE*?

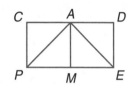

_____ cm²

Explain how you found the area of Triangle *APE.*

_____

_____

_____

197 199

2. Draw a tree diagram for the following problem. Then answer the question.

A bag contains one red counter, two blue counters, and one white counter. You take out one counter. Then you take out a second counter without replacing the first counter. What is the probability of taking out one red counter and one white counter (in either order)?

_____

143 144

3. Multiply.

a. 234
   × 15

b. 784
   × 129

c. 603 * 45

d. 821 * 80

19 20

Plan Your Own Lunch

1. Choose 5 items you would like to have for lunch from the following menu. Choose your favorite foods—pay no attention to calories. Make a check mark next to each item.

Food	Total Calories	Calories from Fat	Calories from Carbohydrate	Calories from Protein
Ham sandwich	265	110	110	45
Turkey sandwich	325	70	155	100
Hamburger	330	135	120	75
Cheeseburger	400	200	110	90
Double burger, cheese, sauce	500	225	175	100
Grilled cheese sandwich	380	220	100	60
Peanut butter and jelly sandwich	380	160	170	50
Chicken nuggets (6)	250	125	65	60
Bagel	165	20	120	25
Bagel with cream cheese	265	105	125	35
Hard-boiled egg	80	55	0	25
French fries (small bag)	250	120	115	15
Apple	100	10	90	0
Carrot	30	0	25	5
Orange	75	0	70	5
Cake (slice)	235	65	160	10
Cashews (1 oz)	165	115	30	20
Doughnut	200	100	75	25
Blueberry muffin	110	30	70	10
Apple pie (slice)	250	125	115	10
Frozen-yogurt cone	100	10	75	15
Orange juice (8 fl oz)	110	0	104	8
2% milk (8 fl oz)	145	45	60	40
Skim milk (8 fl oz)	85	0	50	35
Soft drink (8 fl oz)	140	0	140	0
Diet soft drink (8 fl oz)	0	0	0	0

Use with Lesson 8.5.

Plan Your Own Lunch (cont.)

2. In the table below, record the 5 items you chose. Fill in the rest of the table and write the total number of calories for each column.

Food	Total Calories	Calories from Fat	Calories from Carbohydrate	Calories from Protein
Total				

What percent of the total number of calories in your lunch comes from fat? _____

From carbohydrate? _____   From protein? _____

3. Nutritionists recommend that, at most, 30% of the total number of calories comes from fat, about 12% of the calories from protein, and at least 58% of the calories from carbohydrate.

Does the lunch you chose meet these recommendations? _____

4. Plan another lunch. This time, try to limit the percent of calories from fat to 30% or less, from protein to between 10% and 15%, and from carbohydrate to between 55% and 60%.

Food	Total Calories	Calories from Fat	Calories from Carbohydrate	Calories from Protein
Total				

What percent of the total number of calories in your lunch comes from fat? _____

From carbohydrate? _____   From protein? _____

Unit Percents to Find a Whole

Example 1

The sale price of a CD player is $120, which is 60% of its list price.
What is the list price?

- If 60% of the list price is $120, then 1% is $2. (120 / 60 = 2)

- The list price (the whole or 100%) is $200. (100 * 2 = 200)

Example 2

A toaster is on sale for $40, which is 80% of its list price.
What is the list price?

- If 80% of the list price is $40, then 1% is $0.50. (40 / 80 = 0.5)

- The list price (100%) is $50. (100 * 0.5 = 50)

Use your percent sense to estimate the list price for each item below.
Then calculate the list price. (*Hint:* First use your calculator to find
what 1% is worth.)

Sale Price	Percent of List Price	Estimated List Price	Calculated List Price
$120	60%	$180	$200
$100	50%		
$8	32%		
$255	85%		
$77	55%		
$80	40%		
$9	60%		
$112.50	75%		
$450	90%		

Ratios

Math Message

Work with a partner. You may use a deck of cards to help you with these problems.

1. There are 2 facedown cards for every faceup card.
   If 6 of the cards are faceup, how many cards are facedown? _____ cards

2. You have 12 cards. One out of every 4 cards is faceup.
   The rest are facedown. How many cards are faceup? _____ cards

3. There are 4 facedown cards for every 3 faceup cards.
   If 8 of the cards are facedown, how many cards are faceup? _____ cards

4. Three out of every 5 cards are faceup. If 12
   cards are faceup, how many cards are there in all? _____ cards

5. There are 2 faceup cards for every
   5 facedown. If there are 21 cards
   in all, how many cards are faceup? _____ cards

6. The table at the right shows the average number of
   wet days in selected cities for the month of October.

City	Wet Days
Beijing, China	3
Boston, United States	9
Frankfurt, Germany	14
Mexico City, Mexico	13
Moscow, Russia	15
Sydney, Australia	12

   a. How many more wet days does
      Moscow have than Beijing? _____

   b. Moscow has how many times
      as many wet days as Beijing? _____

   c. The number of wet days in Beijing is what
      fraction of the number of wet days in Sydney? _____

Challenge

7. You have 5 faceup cards and no facedown cards. You add some facedown
   cards so that 1 in every 3 cards is faceup. How many cards are there now? _____ cards

8. You have 5 faceup cards and 12 facedown cards. You add some faceup cards
   so that 2 out of every 5 cards are faceup. How many cards are there now? _____ cards

9. You have 8 faceup cards and 12 facedown cards. You add some faceup cards
   so that $\frac{2}{3}$ of the cards are faceup.

   How many cards are faceup? _____ cards   Facedown? _____ cards

Ratio Number Stories

For each problem, write and solve a proportion.

1. A spinner lands on blue 4 times for every 6 times it lands on green. How many times does it land on green if it lands on blue 12 times?

   a. $\dfrac{\text{lands on blue}}{\text{lands on green}} = \dfrac{\boxed{}}{\boxed{}} = \dfrac{\boxed{}}{\boxed{}}$

   b. It lands on green _____ times.

2. It rained 2 out of 5 days in the month of April. On how many days did it rain that month?

   a. $\dfrac{\text{days with rain}}{\text{days}} = \dfrac{\boxed{}}{\boxed{}} = \dfrac{\boxed{}}{\boxed{}}$

   b. It rained _____ days in April.

3. Of the 42 animals in the Children's Zoo, 3 out of 7 are mammals. How many mammals are there in the Children's Zoo?

   a. $\dfrac{\text{mammals}}{\text{animals}} = \dfrac{\boxed{}}{\boxed{}} = \dfrac{\boxed{}}{\boxed{}}$

   b. Answer _____

4. Last week, Charles spent 2 hours doing homework for every 3 hours he watched TV. If he spent 6 hours doing homework, how many hours did he spend watching TV?

   a. $\dfrac{\boxed{}}{\boxed{}} = \dfrac{\boxed{}}{\boxed{}} = \dfrac{\boxed{}}{\boxed{}}$

   b. Answer _____

5. Five out of 8 students at Lane Junior High School play a musical instrument. 140 students play an instrument. How many students attend Lane School?

   a. $\dfrac{\boxed{}}{\boxed{}} = \dfrac{\boxed{}}{\boxed{}} = \dfrac{\boxed{}}{\boxed{}}$

   b. Answer _____

6. A choir has 50 members. Twenty members are sopranos. How many sopranos are there for every 5 members of the choir?

   a. $\dfrac{\boxed{}}{\boxed{}} = \dfrac{\boxed{}}{\boxed{}} = \dfrac{\boxed{}}{\boxed{}}$

   b. Answer _____

Ratio Number Stories (cont.)

7. Mr. Dexter sells subscriptions to a magazine for $18 each. For each subscription he sells, he earns $8. One month, he sold $900 in subscriptions. How much did he earn?

a.

$$\frac{\boxed{}}{\boxed{}} = \frac{\boxed{}}{\boxed{}} = \frac{\boxed{}}{\boxed{}}$$

b. Answer _____

8. At Kozminski School, the ratio of weeks of school to weeks of vacation is 9 to 4. How many weeks of vacation do students at the school get in one year?

a. Complete the table.

Weeks of school	9	18	27		
Weeks of vacation	4				
Total weeks	13				

b. Write a proportion.

$$\frac{\boxed{}}{\boxed{}} = \frac{\boxed{}}{\boxed{}} = \frac{\boxed{}}{\boxed{}}$$

c. Answer _____

9. The class library has 3 fiction books for every 4 nonfiction books. If the library has a total of 63 books, how many fiction books does it have?

a.

$$\frac{\boxed{}}{\boxed{}} = \frac{\boxed{}}{\boxed{}} = \frac{\boxed{}}{\boxed{}}$$

b. Answer _____

Challenge

10. There are 48 students in the sixth grade at Robert's school. Three out of 8 sixth graders read two books last month. One out of 3 students read just one book. The rest of the students read no books at all. How many books in all did the sixth graders read last month? _____

Tell what you did to solve the problem. _____

_____

_____

_____

_____

Fraction Computation

Solve.

1. $\frac{3}{8} + \frac{11}{12} =$ _____

2. $\frac{4}{7} - \frac{3}{8} =$ _____

3. $3\frac{2}{3} - \frac{7}{9} =$ _____

4. $5\frac{2}{3} + 6\frac{3}{8} =$ _____

5. _____ $= \frac{5}{7} \times \frac{3}{8}$

6. $2\frac{3}{5} * 1\frac{3}{4} =$ _____

7. _____ $= \frac{8}{9} \div \frac{2}{3}$

8. $5\frac{1}{4} / 1\frac{3}{7} =$ _____

9. Explain how you solved Problem 6.

_____

_____

_____

Complete the tables. Write the missing rules. Add your own number pairs to the tables.

10. Rule _____

in	out
$\frac{3}{8}$	$\frac{15}{40}$
$\frac{7}{9}$	$\frac{35}{45}$
	$\frac{80}{100}$
$\frac{6}{7}$	

11. Rule _____

in	out
$\frac{3}{8}$	$\frac{3}{4}$
$\frac{3}{12}$	
	$1\frac{3}{8}$
$\frac{1}{2}$	$\frac{7}{8}$

Use with Lesson 8.6.

Math Boxes 8.6

1. Add or subtract.

a. $14 + (-72) =$ _____

b. _____ $= 27 - (-28)$

c. _____ $= -63 + (-87)$

d. _____ $= -58 + 105$

e. $-33 - (-89) =$ _____

SRB
92 93

2. Circle the equation that describes the relationship between the numbers in the table.

x	y
0.55	$\frac{1}{2}$
0.6	1
1	5
1.5	10

$(y + 0.1) * \frac{1}{2} = x$

$(y * 0.1) + \frac{1}{2} = x$

$\frac{0.1y}{2} = x$

$(y + \frac{1}{2}) * 0.1 = x$

SRB
224 235

3. Which data set below has the following landmarks: range 29, maximum 48, mode 22, median 34? (Circle its letter.)

a.

Stems (10s)	Leaves (1s)
0	
1	9 9
2	1 2 2 2 2 5 7
3	4 6 6 8 9 9
4	2 7 8 8

b.

20	/
22	///
24	//
25	/
34	//
35	//
36	/
37	/
39	//
42	/
48	/

SRB
129 130

4. Evaluate each expression. Use the rules for order of operations.

a. $9 * 5 / 10 + 3 - 2 =$ _____

b. $8 - 6 * 4 + 8 / 2 =$ _____

c. _____ $= 5^2 * 2 + 9 * 2$

d. _____ $= 15 / (2 + 3) - 8 * 2$

e. _____ $= 2 + 2 * 12 + 3^2 - 5$

SRB
229

5. Estimate each product by rounding the larger factor.

a. $19,304,767 * 3$ _____

b. $5 * 29,789,124$ _____

c. $867,259 * 7$ _____

d. $25,483,001 * 40$ _____

SRB
244

Using Proportions to Solve Percent Problems

Math Message

1. In a recent game, the Mansfield School basketball team took 15 three-point shots and made 6 shots. What percent of its shots did the team make? _____

2. The team also took 20 two-point shots and made 45% of them. How many two-point shots did the players make? _____

3. The team made 80% of its free throws (one-point shots). If players made 16 free throws, how many free throws did they attempt? _____

4. How many shots did the team take in all? _____

   How many points did the team score in all? _____

   If your answers are 55 shots and 52 points, then your answers to Problems 2 and 3 are correct.

For each problem, write and solve a proportion.

5. The 12 girls in Ms. Arnold's class make up 40% of the class. How many students are in Ms. Arnold's class?

   a. $\dfrac{\text{girls}}{\text{total}} = \dfrac{\boxed{}}{\boxed{}} = \dfrac{\boxed{}}{\boxed{}}$ b. There are _____ students in Ms. Arnold's class.

6. A sow had a litter with 3 female piglets and 5 male piglets. What percent of piglets are female?

   a. $\dfrac{\text{female}}{\text{total}} = \dfrac{\boxed{}}{\boxed{}} = \dfrac{\boxed{}}{\boxed{}}$ b. _____% of the piglets are female.

7. Matt bought his favorite movie on video for 40% off the regular price. He paid only $18. What was the regular price?

   a. $\dfrac{\text{sale price}}{\text{regular price}} = \dfrac{\boxed{}}{\boxed{}} = \dfrac{\boxed{}}{\boxed{}}$ b. The regular price was $ _____.

   He saved $ _____.

8. In Illinois in 2000, people paid 3% of their income for state tax. What was the tax on an income of $65,000?

   a. $\dfrac{\boxed{}}{\boxed{}} = \dfrac{\boxed{}}{\boxed{}} = \dfrac{\boxed{}}{\boxed{}}$ b. The tax on an income of $65,000 was

   $ _____.

Using Proportions to Solve Percent Problems (cont.)

9. In the 2000 presidential election, California had 54 electoral votes out of a total of 538. What percent of the electoral votes did California have?

a. ⬚/⬚ = ⬚/⬚ = ⬚/⬚   **b.** California had _____% of the electoral votes.

10. Female college graduates earn only about 70% as much as male college graduates. If the average female graduate earns about $40,000 a year, how much does the average male graduate earn?

a. ⬚/⬚ = ⬚/⬚ = ⬚/⬚   **b.** The average male graduate earns about $ _____.

11. In 1999, about 75% of airline flights arrived on time. About how many of the 8.3 million flights arrived on time?

a. ⬚/⬚ = ⬚/⬚ = ⬚/⬚   **b.** About _____ flights were on time.

About _____ flights were late.

12. In 1997, about 9% of eighth grade students smoked daily. About how many of the 3,500,000 eighth graders smoked?

a. ⬚/⬚ = ⬚/⬚ = ⬚/⬚   **b.** About _____ eighth graders smoked.

13. 32% of 50 = _____

part/whole = ⬚/⬚ = ⬚/⬚

14. 15 is 30% of _____.

part/whole = ⬚/⬚ = ⬚/⬚

15. 24 is what percent of 60? _____

part/whole = ⬚/⬚ = ⬚/⬚

16. 36 is what percent of 80? _____

part/whole = ⬚/⬚ = ⬚/⬚

Stem-and-Leaf Plot

1. Construct a stem-and-leaf plot with the following data landmarks.
There should be at least 12 data entries in your plot.

median: 57

minimum: 42

maximum: 78

mode: 60

Stems (10s)	Leaves (1s)

2. Explain how you chose the numbers for your data set.

_____

_____

_____

_____

_____

_____

_____

3. Describe a data set that your stem-and-leaf plot could represent.

_____

_____

_____

_____

Math Boxes 8.7

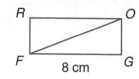

---

1. The area of Triangle *FOG* is 12 cm². What is the perimeter of Rectangle *FROG*?

_____ cm

Explain how you found the perimeter of Rectangle *FROG*.

_____

_____

_____

---

2. Draw a tree diagram for the following problem. Then answer the two questions.

The cafeteria is serving spaghetti, hamburgers, and hot dogs for lunch. The drinks are milk, soda, and juice. If you choose your meal and drink at random, what is the probability of having

a. a hot dog?

_____

b. a hot dog and juice?

_____

---

3. Multiply.

a.   473
      × 95

b.   847
      × 103

c. 624 ∗ 215

d. 704 ∗ 425

The Fat Content of Foods

1. Use the information about calories on each food label below and on the next page.

   a. Write the ratio of calories that come from fat to the total number of calories as a fraction.

   b. Then estimate the percent of total calories that come from fat. Do not use your calculator.

   c. Finally, use your calculator to find the percent of calories that come from fat. (Round to the nearest whole percent.)

Food Label	Food	Calories from Fat / Total Calories	Estimated Fat Percent	Calculated Fat Percent
Nutrition Facts Serving Size 1 slice (28 g) Servings Per Container 12 **Amount Per Serving** **Calories** 90 Calories from Fat 80	bologna	$\frac{80}{90}$	About 90	89%
Nutrition Facts Serving Size 2 waffles (72 g) Servings Per Container 4 **Amount Per Serving** **Calories** 190 Calories from Fat 50	waffle			
Nutrition Facts Serving Size 2 tablespoons (32 g) Servings Per Container 15 **Amount Per Serving** **Calories** 190 Calories from Fat 140	peanut butter			
Nutrition Facts Serving Size 1 slice (19 g) Servings Per Container 24 **Amount Per Serving** **Calories** 70 Calories from Fat 50	American cheese			
Nutrition Facts Serving Size 1 egg (50 g) Servings Per Container 12 **Amount Per Serving** **Calories** 70 Calories from Fat 40	egg			

Use with Lesson 8.8.

The Fat Content of Foods (cont.)

Food Label	Food	Calories from Fat / Total Calories	Estimated Fat Percent	Calculated Fat Percent
Nutrition Facts Serving Size 1 cup (60 mL) Servings Per Container 6 **Amount Per Serving** **Calories** 110 Calories from Fat 0	orange juice			
Nutrition Facts Serving Size 1/2 cup (125 g) Servings Per Container About 3 1/2 **Amount Per Serving** **Calories** 90 Calories from Fat 5	corn			
Nutrition Facts Serving Size 1 package (255 g) Servings Per Container 1 **Amount Per Serving** **Calories** 280 Calories from Fat 90	macaroni and cheese			
Nutrition Facts Serving Size 1/2 cup (106 g) Servings Per Container 4 **Amount Per Serving** **Calories** 270 Calories from Fat 160	ice cream			

2. Compare whole milk to skim (nonfat) milk.

Type of Milk	Total Calories	Calories from Fat	Calories from Carbohydrate	Calories from Protein
1 cup whole milk	160	75	50	35
1 cup skim milk	85	trace	50	35

   a. For whole milk, what percent of the total calories comes from

   fat? _____ %   carbohydrate? _____ %   protein? _____ %

   b. For skim milk, what percent of the total calories comes from

   fat? _____ %   carbohydrate? _____ %   protein? _____ %

3. Find the missing percents.

   a. 25% + 30% + _____ % = 100%   b. 82% + _____ % + 9% = 100%

Circle Graphs

1. Convert the following percents to degree measures on a circle graph.

   a. 27% _____ °   b. 49% _____ °

   c. 73% _____ °   d. 98% _____ °

   e. 65% _____ °

2. Convert the following fractions to degree measures on a circle graph.

   a. $\frac{3}{8}$ _____ °   b. $\frac{6}{9}$ _____ °

   c. $\frac{4}{5}$ _____ °   d. $\frac{8}{12}$ _____ °

   e. $\frac{3}{4}$ _____ °

3. Use your protractor to divide the circle into three sectors by drawing a 48° sector and a 116° sector.

   What is the degree measure of the third sector? _____ °

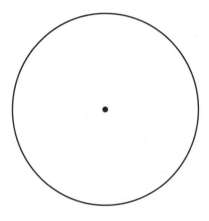

4. Ms. Camponella's sixth graders were having a surprise birthday party for her. The table below shows how many students signed up to bring each kind of treat.

   a. Complete the table.

   b. Use your protractor to make a circle graph that displays the information. Title your graph.

_____
                (title)

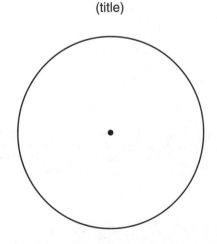

Treat	Number Signed Up	Degree Measure of Sector
Chips	8	
Cookies	5	
Drinks	3	
Fruit	9	

Use with Lesson 8.8.

Math Boxes 8.8

1. Add or subtract.

a. $-303 + (-28) =$ _____

b. _____ $= 245 - 518$

c. _____ $= -73 + 89$

d. _____ $= 176 + (-95)$

e. $280 - (-31) =$ _____

2. Circle the equation that describes the relationship between the numbers in the table.

x	y
1	$\frac{3}{8}$
2	$\frac{3}{4}$
8	3
24	9

$\frac{y}{8} * 3 = x$

$(3 * y) + 8 = x$

$\frac{x}{8} * 3 = y$

$(3 * x) + 8 = y$

3. Which data set below has the following landmarks: maximum 25, minimum 10, mode 18, median 18? (Circle its letter.)

a.

Stems (10s)	Leaves (1s)
0	
1	0 1 1 5 7
2	0 1 3 3 3 5

b.

10	//
11	//
14	///
17	/
18	////
22	//
23	/
25	/

4. Evaluate each expression. Use the rules for order of operations.

a. $3 * 8 / 4 + 7 =$ _____

b. $9 + 3 * 5 - 7 =$ _____

c. _____ $= 6 * 5 + 7 * 3$

d. _____ $= 8 / (2 + 8) * 3^3 + 5$

e. _____ $= 28 - 7 * 4 * 0 + 2$

5. Estimate each product by rounding the larger factor to the nearest million.

a. $65,002,389 * 2$ _____

b. $3 * 300,894,115$ _____

c. $15,224,025 \times 5$ _____

d. $501,444 \times 70$ _____

Use with Lesson 8.8.

321

Enlargements

A copy machine was used to make a 2X enlargement of shapes on the Geometry Template.

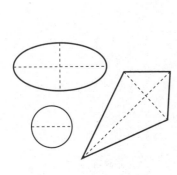
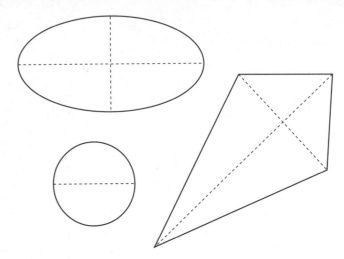

1. Use your ruler to measure the line segments shown in the figures above to the nearest $\frac{1}{16}$ inch. Then fill in the table below.

Line Segment	Length of Original	Length of Enlargement	Ratio of Enlargement to Original
Diameter of circle			
Longer axis of ellipse			
Shorter axis of ellipse			
Longer side of kite			
Shorter side of kite			
Longer diagonal of kite			
Shorter diagonal of kite			

2. Are the figures in the enlargement similar to the original figures? _____

3. What does a 3.5X enlargement mean? _____

_____

_____

_____

Use with Lesson 8.9.

Map Scale

This map shows the downtown area of the city of Chicago. The shaded area shows the part of Chicago that was destroyed in the Chicago fire of 1871.

The map was drawn to a scale of 1:50,000. This means that each 1-inch length on the map represents 50,000 inches (about $\frac{3}{4}$ mile) of actual distance.

$$\frac{\text{map distance}}{\text{actual distance}} = \frac{1}{50,000}$$

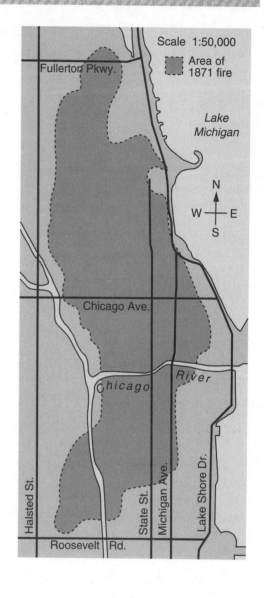

Scale 1:50,000

Area of 1871 fire

1. Measure the distance on the map between Fullerton Parkway and Roosevelt Road, to the nearest $\frac{1}{4}$ inch. This is the approximate north-south length of the part that burned.

    Burn length on map = _____ inches

2. Measure the width of the part that burned, along Chicago Avenue, to the nearest $\frac{1}{4}$ inch. This is the approximate east-west length of the part that burned.

    Burn width on map = _____ inches

3. Use the map scale to find the actual length and width of the part of Chicago that burned.

    a. Actual burn length = _____ inches

    b. Actual burn width = _____ inches

4. Convert the answers in Problem 3 from inches to miles, to the nearest tenth of a mile.

    a. Actual burn length = _____ miles

    b. Actual burn width = _____ miles

5. Estimate the area of the part of Chicago that burned, to the nearest square mile.

    Area of part that burned   About _____ square miles

Rounding Quotients

Divide. Show your work in the space below.
In Problems 1–3, round your answers to the nearest tenth.

1. 97.6 ÷ 6 = _____

2. 74.9 / 32 = _____

3. 864.9 ÷ 15 = _____

In Problems 4–6, round your answers to the nearest hundredth.

4. 587.48 / 9 = _____

5. 307.4 ÷ 7 = _____

6. 696.1 / 68 = _____

7. Explain how you rounded the answer in Problem 6.

_____

_____

_____

_____

Use with Lesson 8.9.

Math Boxes 8.9

---

1. The spreadsheet shows how Jonas spent his money for the first quarter of the year.

a. In which cell is the largest amount that Jonas spent?

_____

	A	B	C	D	E
1	Month	January	February	March	Total
2	Food	15.28	19.14	10.04	
3	Movies	10.00	14.00	5.00	

b. Calculate the values for Cells E2 and E3 and enter them on the spreadsheet.

c. Circle the correct formula for figuring out how much money Jonas spent in February.

D1 + D2 + D3   C2 + C3   B3 + C3 + D3

SRB
137 138

---

2. Multiply or divide.

a. −8 * 6 = _____

b. 550 / (−11) = _____

c. _____ = −125 / (−5)

d. _____ = −930 / 31

e. _____ = −500 * 40

SRB
95

---

3. Complete.

a. 19 qt = _____ pt

b. 9 gal 3 pt = _____ c

c. _____ pt _____ c = 27 c

d. _____ c = 43 pt

e. 560 c = _____ qt

SRB
201

---

4. Complete the Venn diagram.

Name at least two ways in which the numbers 18 and 27 are alike.

Name at least two ways in which they are different.

18   27

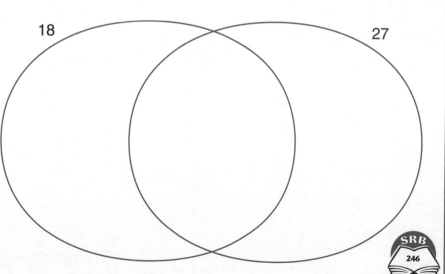

SRB
246

Similar Polygons

1. Use pattern-block trapezoids to construct a trapezoid whose sides are twice the length of the corresponding sides of a single pattern-block trapezoid. Then use your Geometry Template to record what you did.

2. Draw a trapezoid whose sides are 3 times the length of a single pattern-block trapezoid. You may use any drawing or measuring tools you wish, such as a compass, a ruler, a protractor, the trapezoid on your Geometry Template, or a trapezoid pattern block.

    Which tools did you use? _____

3. Cover the trapezoid you drew in Problem 2 with pattern-block trapezoids. Then use your Geometry Template to record the way you covered the trapezoid.

Use with Lesson 8.10.

Similar Polygons (cont.)

4. Measure line segments *AB, CD,* and *EF* with a centimeter ruler. Draw a line segment *GH* so that the ratio of the lengths of *AB* to *CD* is equal to the ratio of the lengths of *EF* to *GH*.

$$\frac{\text{length of } \overline{AB}}{\text{length of } \overline{CD}} = \frac{\text{length of } \overline{EF}}{\text{length of } \overline{GH}}$$

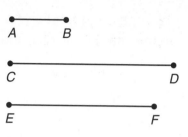

5. Pentagons *PAINT* and *MODEL* are similar polygons. Find the missing lengths of sides.

   a. Length of side *MO* =

   _____ units

   b. Length of side *EL* =

   _____ units

   c. Length of side *DE* =

   _____ units

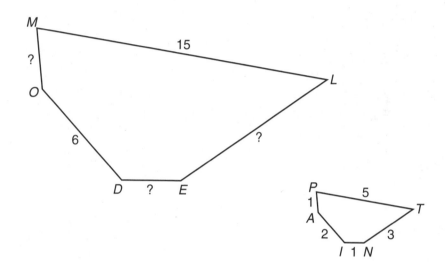

6. Triangles *PAL* and *CUT* are similar figures. Find the missing lengths of sides.

   a. Length of side *AL* = _____ units

   b. Length of side *UT* = _____ units

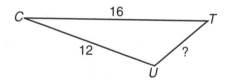

7. Alexi is looking at a map of his town. The scale given on the map is 1 inch represents $\frac{1}{2}$ mile. Alexi measures the distance from his home to school on the map—it's $3\frac{3}{4}$ inches. What is the actual distance from his home to school?

   _____ miles

8. For a school fair in the cafeteria, Nina wants to construct a scale model of the 984-foot-tall Eiffel Tower. She plans to use a scale of 1 to 6—every length of the scale model will be $\frac{1}{6}$ of the actual size of the Eiffel Tower. Does this scale seem reasonable? If yes, explain why. If no, suggest a more reasonable scale.

_____

_____

Renaming Fractions as Decimals

Rename each fraction as a decimal, rounded to the nearest hundredth, by dividing the numerator by the denominator.

Example $\frac{3}{7} = ?$

Step 1 Estimate the quotient: $\frac{3}{7}$ is a little less than $\frac{1}{2}$; so $\frac{3}{7}$ is a little less than 0.50.

Step 2 To get two decimals places in the quotient, rewrite 3 as 3.00; $\frac{3}{7} = \frac{3.00}{7}$

Step 3 Divide, ignoring the decimal point.

Step 4 Use the estimate to place the decimal point in your quotient: 0.42

Step 5 Round the answer: Since the remainder, 6, is more than half of the dividend, 7, round up: 0.43

$$\begin{array}{r|l} 7)\overline{300} & \\ -\ 280 & 40 \\ \hline 20 & \\ -\ 14 & 2 \\ \hline 6 & 42 \end{array}$$

1. $\frac{5}{7}$ **a.** Estimate _____

          b. Answer _____

2. $\frac{8}{9}$ **a.** Estimate _____

          b. Answer _____

3. $\frac{5}{6}$ **a.** Estimate _____

          b. Answer _____

4. $\frac{2}{15}$ **a.** Estimate _____

          b. Answer _____

Challenge

5. $\frac{15}{16}$ **a.** Estimate _____

          b. Answer _____

6. Explain what you would do to find the decimal equivalent for $\frac{3}{7}$ to the thousandths place (three decimal places).

_____

_____

Math Boxes 8.10

1. The formula $d = rt$ gives the distance d traveled at speed r in time t.
Use this formula to solve the problems below.

    a. Ms. Ruiz is driving at an average speed of 60 miles
per hour. At this speed, how far can she drive in 4.5 hours? _____

    b. Jill walks at an average speed of 5 miles per hour.
At this speed, how far can she walk in 2.5 hours? _____

    c. The distance from San Francisco to Los Angeles
is about 420 miles. About how many hours will it
take to drive from San Francisco to Los Angeles
at an average speed of 55 miles per hour? _____

SRB
227 228

---

2. Multiply or divide. Write your answer in simplest form.

    a. $\frac{8}{9} \div \frac{4}{5} =$ _____

    b. $3\frac{8}{5} * \frac{2}{3} =$ _____

    c. _____ $= 5\frac{1}{2} \div \frac{11}{12}$

    d. _____ $= \frac{29}{4} * \frac{15}{6}$

    e. _____ $= \frac{3}{7} * 18$

SRB
86 89

3. Write five names for the number in the name-collection box so that each name includes the number (-2) and subtraction.

10

SRB
93 95

---

4. Write each number in standard notation. Then round it to the nearest tenth.

    a. four and sixty-two thousandths

    standard notation _____

    rounded _____

    b. three and eighty-eight hundredths

    standard notation _____

    rounded _____

    c. two hundred seventy thousandths

    standard notation _____

    rounded _____

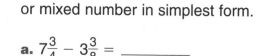
SRB
27 54

5. Subtract. Write your answer as a fraction or mixed number in simplest form.

    a. $7\frac{3}{4} - 3\frac{3}{8} =$ _____

    b. _____ $= \frac{5}{2} - 1\frac{5}{6}$

    c. _____ $= 5\frac{1}{3} - 2\frac{5}{9}$

    d. _____ $= 17 - 13\frac{4}{5}$

    e. $8\frac{2}{3} - 4\frac{7}{9} =$ _____

SRB
81 82

Renaming and Comparing Ratios

Use the data you collected on Study Link 8.8. Use your calculator.
Round to the nearest tenth.

1. The ratio of left-handed to right-handed people in my household

$$\frac{\text{left-handed}}{\text{right-handed}} = \frac{\boxed{}}{\boxed{}} \quad \text{is about} \quad \frac{\boxed{}}{1}$$

2. The ratio of the length of the American flag I found to its width

$$\frac{\text{flag length}}{\text{flag width}} = \frac{\boxed{}}{\boxed{}} \quad \text{is about} \quad \frac{\boxed{}}{1}$$

3. The ratio of the length of the screen of my TV set to its width

$$\frac{\text{TV length}}{\text{TV width}} = \frac{\boxed{}}{\boxed{}} \quad \text{is about} \quad \frac{\boxed{}}{1}$$

4. a. The ratio of the length of a small book to its width

$$\frac{\text{small book length}}{\text{small book width}} = \frac{\boxed{}}{\boxed{}} \quad \text{is about} \quad \frac{\boxed{}}{1}$$

   b. The ratio of the length of a medium book to its width

$$\frac{\text{medium book length}}{\text{medium book width}} = \frac{\boxed{}}{\boxed{}} \quad \text{is about} \quad \frac{\boxed{}}{1}$$

   c. The ratio of the length of a large book to its width

$$\frac{\text{large book length}}{\text{large book width}} = \frac{\boxed{}}{\boxed{}} \quad \text{is about} \quad \frac{\boxed{}}{1}$$

   d. What is the shape of a book with a length to width ratio of 1 to 1? _____

5. a. The ratio of the length of a postcard to its width

$$\frac{\text{postcard length}}{\text{postcard width}} = \frac{\boxed{}}{\boxed{}} \quad \text{is about} \quad \frac{\boxed{}}{1}$$

   b. The ratio of the length of an index card to its width

$$\frac{\text{index card length}}{\text{index card width}} = \frac{\boxed{}}{\boxed{}} \quad \text{is about} \quad \frac{\boxed{}}{1}$$

   c. The ratio of the length of a regular-size envelope to its width

$$\frac{\text{envelope length}}{\text{envelope width}} = \frac{\boxed{}}{\boxed{}} \quad \text{is about} \quad \frac{\boxed{}}{1}$$

   d. The ratio of the length of a business envelope to its width

$$\frac{\text{business envelope length}}{\text{business envelope width}} = \frac{\boxed{}}{\boxed{}} \quad \text{is about} \quad \frac{\boxed{}}{1}$$

   e. The ratio of the length of a sheet of notebook paper to its width

$$\frac{\text{notebook paper length}}{\text{notebook paper width}} = \frac{\boxed{}}{\boxed{}} \quad \text{is about} \quad \frac{\boxed{}}{1}$$

Use with Lesson 8.11.

6. Measure the length and width of each rectangle in Problem 6 on Study Link 8.8. to the nearest tenth of a centimeter. Find the ratio of length to width for each rectangle.

a. $\dfrac{\text{length of A}}{\text{width of A}} = \dfrac{\boxed{}}{\boxed{}} = \dfrac{\boxed{}}{1}$

b. $\dfrac{\text{length of B}}{\text{width of B}} = \dfrac{\boxed{}}{\boxed{}} = \dfrac{\boxed{}}{1}$

c. $\dfrac{\text{length of C}}{\text{width of C}} = \dfrac{\boxed{}}{\boxed{}} = \dfrac{\boxed{}}{1}$

d. $\dfrac{\text{length of D}}{\text{width of D}} = \dfrac{\boxed{}}{\boxed{}} = \dfrac{\boxed{}}{1}$

e. Which of the four rectangles was the most popular? _____

7. The ratio of the rise to the run of my stairs is $\dfrac{\text{rise}}{\text{run}} = \dfrac{\boxed{}}{\boxed{}} = \dfrac{\boxed{}}{1}$

Share the data you recorded in Problems 1–7 with the other members of your group. Use these data to answer the following questions.

8. Which group member has the largest ratio of left-handed people to right-handed people at home? _____ What is this ratio? _____

9. By law, the length of an official United States flag must be 1.9 times its width.

a. Did the flag you measured meet this standard? _____

b. What percent of the flags measured by your group meets this standard? _____

c. Why do you think such a law exists? _____

_____

d. One of the largest United States flags was displayed at the J.L. Hudson store in Detroit, Michigan. The flag was 235 feet by 104 feet. Does this flag meet the legal requirements? _____

e. How can you tell? _____

_____

10. a. For most television sets, the ratio of the length to the width of the screen is about 4 to 3. Is this true of the television sets in your group? _____

b. Why do you think it is important to have similar ratios of length to width for TV screens?

_____

_____

Renaming and Comparing Ratios (cont.)

11. Compare the ratios for small, medium, and large books measured by your group.

Which size books tends to have
the largest ratio of length to width? _____

Which size tends to have the smallest ratio? _____

12. It is often claimed that the "nicest looking" rectangular shapes have a special ratio
of length to width. Such rectangles are called **Golden Rectangles.** In a Golden
Rectangle, the ratio of length to width is about 8 to 5.

A   B   C   D

a. Which of the four rectangles—A, B, C, or D—is
closest to having the shape of a Golden Rectangle? _____

b. Did most people in your family
choose the Golden Rectangle? _____

c. Draw a Golden Rectangle whose
shorter sides are 2 centimeters long.

d. Are any of the items in Problem 5
on page 330 Golden Rectangles? _____

If so, which ones are they? _____

13. Most stairs in homes have a rise of about
7 inches and a run of about $10\frac{1}{2}$ inches.
Therefore, the rise is about $\frac{2}{3}$ of the run.

a. Is this true of your stairs? _____

b. Which stairs would be steeper, stairs
with a rise-to-run ratio of 2:3 or 3:2?

_____

c. Which member of your group has the

steepest stairs? _____

What is the ratio of rise to run? _____

d. On the grid at the right, draw stairs
whose rise is $\frac{2}{5}$ of the run.

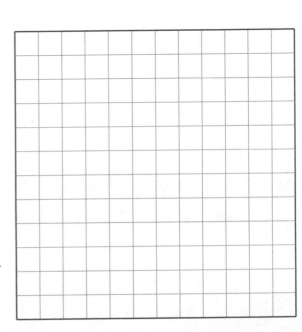

Use with Lesson 8.11 .

Decimal Divisors

First, estimate the answer. Write a number model for the estimate. Then divide, ignoring the decimal points. Finally, use your estimate to place the decimal point in the answer. Show your work in the space below each problem.

1. 18.86 ÷ 2.3

Estimate _____

Answer _____

2. 326.86 ÷ 5.9

Estimate _____

Answer _____

3. 28.81 / 4.3

Estimate _____

Answer _____

4. 23.033 ÷ 3.1

Estimate _____

Answer _____

5. 15.5 / 0.5

Estimate _____

Answer _____

6. 378 ÷ 2.4

Estimate _____

Answer _____

Math Boxes 8.11

---

1. The spreadsheet shows Cecilia's utility bills for two months.

	A	B	C	D	E
1	Month	Phone	Electric	Gas	Total
2	January	$17.95	$38.50	$120.50	
3	February	$34.70	$35.60	$148.96	

   a. If Cecilia entered the wrong electric bill for February, which cell should she correct?

     _____

   b. Calculate the values for Cells E2 and E3 and enter them on the spreadsheet.

   c. Circle the correct formula for figuring out the total cost of utilities in February.

     A2 + B2 + C2 + D2   B3 + C3 + D3   (B2 +C2 + D2) / 3

---

2. Multiply or divide.

   a. $-35 * 16 =$ _____

   b. $240 / -3 =$ _____

   c. _____ $= -840 / -40$

   d. _____ $= 25 * -32$

   e. _____ $= -199 * -12$

3. Complete.

   a. 10 qt = _____ pt

   b. 7 gal 3 qt = _____ pt

   c. _____ pt = 48 c

   d. _____ gal _____ qt = 43 pt

   e. 40 c = _____ gal

---

4. Complete the Venn diagram.

Name at least two ways in which the numbers 21 and 14 are alike.

Name at least two ways in which they are different.

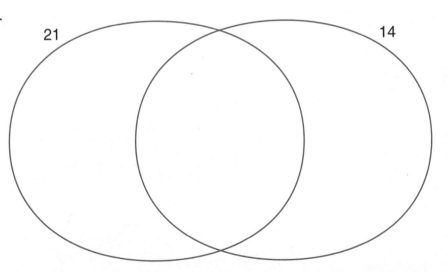

21   14

Date _____ Time _____

Rectangle Length-to-Width Ratios

1. Draw a large rectangle.

2. Measure the length and width of your rectangle to the nearest centimeter. Calculate the ratio of length to width. (Call the longer side the length and the shorter side the width.)

$$\frac{\text{length}}{\text{width}} = \frac{\boxed{}}{\boxed{}} = \frac{\boxed{}}{1}$$

3. Using a compass, draw two arcs on your rectangle as shown: The arcs are drawn with the compass point at vertices that are next to each other. The compass opening is the same for both arcs.

4. Connect the ends of your arcs to make a square. Shade the square. Your rectangle should now look something like this:

5. Measure the length and width of the unshaded part of your rectangle to the nearest centimeter. Calculate the ratio of the length of the rectangle to its width. (As before, call the longer side the length and the shorter side the width.)

$$\frac{\text{length}}{\text{width}} = \frac{\boxed{}}{\boxed{}} = \frac{\boxed{}}{1}$$

6. Are the ratios you calculated in Problems 2 and 5 equal? _____

Use with Lesson 8.12.

Length-to-Width Ratios in a Golden Rectangle

1. Measure the length and width of Rectangle *ABCD* to the nearest tenth of a centimeter. (Call the longer side the length and the shorter side the width.) Calculate the length to width ratio to the nearest tenth.

$$\frac{\text{length}}{\text{width}} = \frac{\boxed{}}{\boxed{}} = \frac{\boxed{}}{1}$$

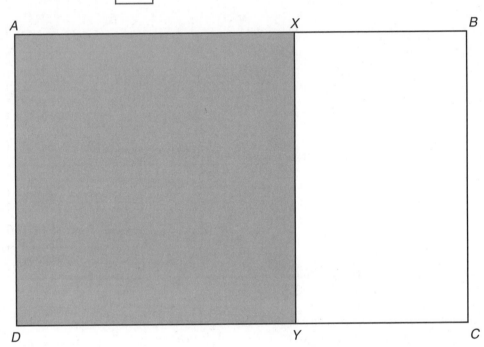

2. Measure the sides of Rectangle *AXYD*. What kind of rectangle is *AXYD*?

_____

3. Measure the length and width of Rectangle *XBCY*. (Call the longer side the length and the shorter side the width.) Calculate the length to width ratio.

$$\frac{\text{length}}{\text{width}} = \frac{\boxed{}}{\boxed{}} = \frac{\boxed{}}{1}$$

4. What do you notice about the ratios you calculated in Problems 1 and 3?

_____

_____

_____

Use with Lesson 8.12.

Math Boxes 8.12

---

1. The formula $d = rt$ gives the distance d traveled at speed r in time t.
   Use this formula to solve the problems below.

   a. The distance from Chicago to Los Angeles is about 2,190 miles.
   About how many hours will it take to drive from Chicago to
   Los Angeles at an average speed of 55 miles per hour? _____

   b. About how long will an airplane flying at an average
   speed of 500 miles per hour take to travel this distance? _____

   c. Circle the formula that is equivalent to $d = rt$.

   $r = d / t$ $r = d - t$ $r = t / d$ $r = t + d$

---

2. Multiply or divide. Write your answer in simplest form.

   a. $\frac{3}{8} \div \frac{6}{7} =$ _____

   b. $1\frac{2}{3} * \frac{4}{5} =$ _____

   c. _____ $= \frac{6}{2} \div \frac{9}{11}$

   d. _____ $= 3\frac{3}{9} * \frac{2}{11}$

   e. _____ $= 5\frac{1}{5} * 8$

3. Write five names for the number in the name-collection box so that each name contains the fraction $\frac{1}{3}$ and includes multiplication.

---

4. Write each number in standard notation. Then round to the nearest tenth.

   a. six and twenty-nine hundredths

   standard notation _____

   rounded _____

   b. four and thirteen ten-thousandths

   standard notation _____

   rounded _____

   c. fourteen and sixty-two hundredths

   standard notation _____

   rounded _____

5. Subtract. Write your answer as a fraction or mixed number in simplest form.

   a. $\frac{3}{2} - \frac{5}{8} =$ _____

   b. _____ $= 4\frac{2}{3} - 1\frac{1}{2}$

   c. _____ $= 3\frac{1}{4} - 1\frac{5}{6}$

   d. $5\frac{8}{9} - \frac{25}{25} =$ _____

Time to Reflect

1. Name at least four ways we use ratios or rates in everyday life.

_____

_____

_____

_____

_____

_____

2. How would you explain the word *ratio* to a new student who had not studied ratios before?

_____

_____

_____

_____

_____

_____

_____

3. Describe the most difficult thing about solving rate and ratio problems.

_____

_____

_____

_____

_____

_____

_____

Use with Lesson 8.13.

1. Insert parentheses to make each equation true.

a. $\frac{1}{2} * 18 + 2 * 15 = 150$

b. $\frac{1}{2} * 18 + 2 * 15 = 39$

c. $5 / 3 + 3 * 5 = 4\frac{1}{6}$

d. $0.8 * 20 + 10 * 0.7 = 23$

e. $4 / 9 + 3 * 6 = 2$

2. The circumference of a circle is given by the formula $C = \pi * d$, where C is the circumference and d is the diameter. Circle an equivalent formula.

$d = C / \pi$ $d = C * \pi$

$d = \pi / C$ $d = \pi + C$

Find the circumference for a circle with a diameter of 5 cm.

_____ cm

3. Mr. and Mrs. Gauss keep a record of their expenses on a spreadsheet.

a. If the Gausses entered the wrong amount for car expenses in July, which cell should they correct? _____

b. In which month were the total expenses greater? _____

How much greater? _____

	A	B	C
1	Total of Expense	June	July
2	Rent and Utilities	$755	$723
3	Food	$125	$189
4	Car Expenses	$179	$25
5	Clothing	$65	$0
6	Miscellaneous	$45	$23
7	Total		

c. Circle the correct formula for the total for June.

A7 + B7 + C7   B2 + B3 + B4 + B5 + B6   (B2 + B3 + B4 + B5 + B6) / 5

4. Solve the equation.

$-47 + 6z = 3z - 2$

Solution _____

5. Add or subtract.

a. $235 + (-150) =$ _____

b. $-76 - 24 =$ _____

c. _____ $= 143 - 258$

d. _____ $= -99 + 167$

e. _____ $= 380 - (-59)$

Two Methods for Finding Areas of Rectangles

Math Message

1. What is the area of Rectangle A? _____ square units

Rectangle A

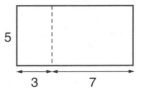

We can express the area of Rectangle A with a number sentence in four ways.

$5 * (3 + 7) = 50$ $(5 * 3) + (5 * 7) = 50$

$(3 + 7) * 5 = 50$ $(3 * 5) + (7 * 5) = 50$

---

2. Write a number sentence for the area of Rectangle B in two ways.

Rectangle B

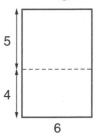

_____ * (_____ + _____) = _____

(_____ * _____) + (_____ * _____) = _____

3. The area of Rectangle C is 144 square units.

a. What is the value of x? _____

Rectangle C

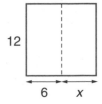

b. Write a number sentence for the area of Rectangle C in two ways.

_____ * (_____ + _____) = 144

(_____ * _____) + (_____ * _____) = 144

4. Each of the following expressions describes the area of one of the rectangles below. Write the letter of the rectangle next to the expression.

Rectangle D

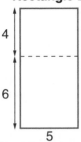

Rectangle E

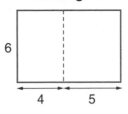

Rectangle F

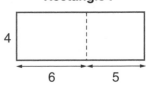

a. $6 * (5 + 4)$ ___*E*___   **b.** $(4 + 6) * 5$ _____

c. 44 _____   **d.** $24 + 30$ _____

e. $(6 * 4) + (5 * 4)$ _____   **f.** 50 _____

g. $(5 * 6) + (4 * 6)$ _____   **h.** $24 + 20$ _____

i. $(6 + 5) * 4$ _____   **j.** $(5 * 6) + (5 * 4)$ _____

Use with Lesson 9.1.

Two Methods for Finding Areas of Rectangles (cont.)

5. What is the area of the shaded part of Rectangle G?

Area of shaded part = _____ square units

We can express the area of the shaded part of
Rectangle G with a number sentence in four ways.

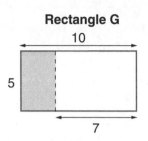

Rectangle G

$5 * (10 - 7) = 15$ $(5 * 10) - (5 * 7) = 15$

$(10 - 7) * 5 = 15$ $(10 * 5) - (7 * 5) = 15$

6. Write a number sentence for the area of the shaded part
of Rectangle H in two ways.

_____ * (_____ − _____) = _____

(_____ * _____) − (_____ * _____) = _____

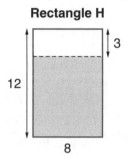

Rectangle H

7. The area of Rectangle I is 48 square units.

  a. What is the value of y? _____

  b. Write a number sentence for the area of the shaded part
     of Rectangle I in two ways.

    (_____ − _____) * _____ = 30

    (_____ * _____) − (_____ * _____) = 30

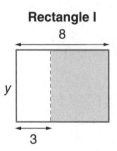

Rectangle I

8. Each of the following expressions describes the area of the shaded part of one of
the rectangles below. Write the letter of the rectangle next to the expression.

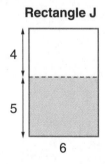

Rectangle J

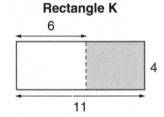

Rectangle K

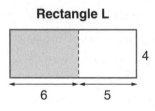

Rectangle L

  a. $4 * (11 - 6)$ _____   **b.** $44 - 20$ _____

  c. 30 _____   **d.** $(6 * 9) - (6 * 4)$ _____

  e. $(4 * 11) - (4 * 6)$ _____   **f.** $(11 - 5) * 4$ _____

  g. $(11 * 4) - (5 * 4)$ _____   **h.** $6 * (9 - 4)$ _____

Math Boxes 9.1

1. a. Draw an obtuse angle *CAT*. Measure it.

b. Draw a reflex angle *NOD.* Measure it.

∠*CAT* measures about _____°.

∠*NOD* measures about _____°.

148
212 213

---

2. Divide.

9,755 / 82 → _____

22–24

---

3. Divide.

a. $\frac{3}{7} \div \frac{4}{5} =$ _____

b. $\frac{8}{12} \div \frac{2}{3} =$ _____

c. $\frac{9}{8} \div \frac{6}{5} =$ _____

d. $\frac{7}{10} \div \frac{2}{1} =$ _____

e. $7 \div \frac{4}{5} =$ _____

89 90

---

4. Circle the equation that describes the relationship between the numbers in the table.

$(x - 9) * 5 = y$

$\frac{x - 9}{5} = y$

$(y + 5) * 9 = x$

$5 * (y + 5) = x$

x	y
10	$\frac{1}{5}$
14	1
19	2
49	8

224 225
235

---

5. Evaluate each expression. Use the rules for order of operations.

a. $9 - 3 * 2 =$ _____

b. $-7 * 6 \div (-3) =$ _____

c. $0.3 + 2^2 * 8 =$ _____

d. $11 - 2.2 * 4 + 7 =$ _____

e. $8 + \frac{1}{6} - 2 =$ _____

224 229

Use with Lesson 9.1.

The Distributive Property

The distributive property is a number property that combines multiplication with addition or multiplication with subtraction. The distributive property can be stated in four different ways.

Multiplication over Addition	**Multiplication over Subtraction**
For any numbers a, x, and y:	For any numbers a, x, and y:
$a * (x + y) = (a * x) + (a * y)$	$a * (x - y) = (a * x) - (a * y)$
$(x + y) * a = (x * a) + (y * a)$	$(x - y) * a = (x * a) - (y * a)$

Use the distributive property to fill in the blanks.

1. $4 * (70 + 8) = (4 * \underline{\hspace{1cm}}) + (4 * \underline{\hspace{1cm}})$

2. $6 * 34 = (\underline{\hspace{1cm}} * 30) + (\underline{\hspace{1cm}} * 4)$

3. $(6 * 70) - (6 * 4) = \underline{\hspace{1cm}} * (70 - \underline{\hspace{1cm}})$

4. $(\underline{\hspace{1cm}} + \underline{\hspace{1cm}}) * 8 = (40 * 8) + (6 * \underline{\hspace{1cm}})$

5. $y * (90 + 3) = (\underline{\hspace{1cm}} * 90) + (y * 3)$

6. $(50 * 7) + (8 * \underline{\hspace{1cm}}) = (\underline{\hspace{1cm}} + \underline{\hspace{1cm}}) * 7$

7. $9 * (20 - 7) = (9 * \underline{\hspace{1cm}}) - (\underline{\hspace{1cm}} * 7)$

8. $(18 - 4) * r = (18 * \underline{\hspace{1cm}}) - (\underline{\hspace{1cm}} * r)$

9. $7 * (w - \underline{\hspace{1cm}}) = (\underline{\hspace{1cm}} * w) - (\underline{\hspace{1cm}} * 6)$

10. $4 * (5 + 6) = (\underline{\hspace{1cm}} * \underline{\hspace{1cm}}) + (\underline{\hspace{1cm}} * \underline{\hspace{1cm}})$

11. $(41 + 19) * 7 = (\underline{\hspace{1cm}} * \underline{\hspace{1cm}}) + (\underline{\hspace{1cm}} * \underline{\hspace{1cm}})$

12. $n * (13 - 27) = (\underline{\hspace{1cm}} * \underline{\hspace{1cm}}) - (\underline{\hspace{1cm}} * \underline{\hspace{1cm}})$

13. $(f - 8) * 15 = (\underline{\hspace{1cm}} * \underline{\hspace{1cm}}) - (\underline{\hspace{1cm}} * \underline{\hspace{1cm}})$

14. $(29 * x) + (12 * x) = (\underline{\hspace{1cm}} + \underline{\hspace{1cm}}) * \underline{\hspace{1cm}}$

15. $6 * (d - 7) = \underline{\hspace{4cm}}$

16. $5 * (12 - h) = \underline{\hspace{4cm}}$

Math Boxes 9.2

1. Mr. Wilson's 28 sixth graders had to read at least one nonfiction book—either a biography or a science book. At the end of the grading period, Mr. Wilson tallied the number of students who had read each kind of book. Nineteen had read at least one biography, and 18 had read at least one science book.

Draw a Venn diagram to represent the number of students who read each kind of book.

How many students read at least one biography and one science book? _____

SRB
246

2. Write >, <, or =.

   a. 28 + (−15) _____ 36 ÷ (−2)

   b. $\frac{1}{2} + (-\frac{3}{4})$ _____ $\frac{2}{3} * \frac{7}{8}$

   c. −400 * −3 _____ 20^2

   d. 2 + 15 / 3 _____ $7 * 10^{-1}$

   e. $\frac{3}{7} + 6\frac{2}{3}$ _____ $\frac{12}{2} \div \frac{7}{9}$

SRB
9

3. Regina got 90% of her spelling test correct.

   a. How many questions did she get right out of 50?

   _____

   b. Write a proportion to solve the problem.

   _____

SRB
59 60

4. Multiply. Write each answer in simplest form.

   a. $7\frac{1}{5} * \frac{3}{8}$ = _____

   b. _____ = $2\frac{4}{9} * 1\frac{1}{5}$

   c. _____ = $1\frac{1}{6} * \frac{7}{6}$

   d. _____ = $5\frac{2}{3} * 4\frac{1}{4}$

   e. $9 * \frac{8}{7}$ = _____

SRB
86

5. Complete.

   a. $33\frac{1}{3}$% of 222 = _____

   b. 25% of 648 = _____

   c. _____ = 40% of 525

   d. _____ = 12.5% of 72

   e. _____ = 70% of 110

SRB
57

Math Boxes 9.3

1. Measure the angles.

a.

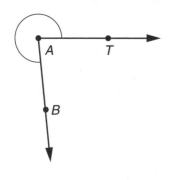

Reflex ∠*BAT* measures about _____ .°

b.

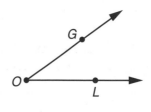

∠*LOG* measures about _____ .°

---

2. Divide.

4,791 / 24 → _____

3. Divide.

a. $\frac{3}{2} \div \frac{3}{9} =$ _____

b. $\frac{7}{8} \div \frac{2}{3} =$ _____

c. $\frac{5}{6} \div \frac{1}{5} =$ _____

d. $\frac{4}{7} \div \frac{9}{12} =$ _____

e. $6 \div \frac{3}{8} =$ _____

---

4. Circle the equation that describes the relationship between the numbers in the table.

$(x * 4) - 3 = y$

$(4 * x) + 3 = y$

$(y * 5) - 3 = x$

$(4 * y) + 3 = x$

x	y
$\frac{1}{4}$	−2
$\frac{1}{2}$	−1
4	13
10	37

5. Evaluate each expression. Use the rules for order of operations.

a. $8 + 5.5 * 7 =$ _____

b. $9 - 6^2 / 3 =$ _____

c. $6 * -4 / -2 =$ _____

d. $5 * 8 - (4 + 2 / 3) =$ _____

e. $4 - 10 + 7 * (-2) =$ _____

Combining Like Terms

Algebraic expressions contain **terms.** For example, the expression $4y + 2x - 7y$
contains the terms $4y$, $2x$, and $7y$. The terms $4y$ and $7y$ are called **like terms**
because they are multiples of the same variable, y. To **combine like terms** means
to rewrite the sum or difference of like terms as a single term. For example, $4y + 7y$
can be rewritten as $11y$.

To **simplify an expression** means to write the expression in a simpler form. Combining
like terms is one way to do that. *Reminder:* The multiplication symbol ($*$) is often not
written. For example, $4 * y$ is often written as $4y$, and $(x + 3) * 5$ as $(x + 3)5$.

Example 1 Simplify the expression $5x - (-8)x$. Use the distributive property.

$$5x - (-8)x = (5 * x) - (-8 * x)$$
$$= (5 - (-8)) * x$$
$$= (5 + 8) * x$$
$$= 13 * x, \text{ or } 13x$$

Check your answer by substituting several values for the variable.

Check: Substitute 5 for the variable.   Check: Substitute 2 for the variable.

$$5x - (-8)x = 13x \qquad\qquad 5x - (-8)x = 13x$$
$$(5 * 5) - (-8 * 5) = 13 * 5 \qquad (5 * 2) - (-8 * 2) = 13 * 2$$
$$25 - (-40) = 65 \qquad\qquad 10 - (-16) = 26$$
$$65 = 65 \qquad\qquad\qquad 26 = 26$$

If there are more than two like terms, you can add or subtract the terms in the order
in which they occur and keep a running total.

Example 2 Simplify the expression $2n - 7n + 3n - 4n$.

$$2n - 7n = -5n$$
$$-5n + 3n = -2n$$
$$-2n - 4n = -6n$$

Therefore, $2n - 7n + 3n - 4n = -6n$

Simplify each expression by rewriting it as a single term.

1. $6y + 13y =$ _____

2. $7g - 12g =$ _____

3. _____ $= 5\frac{1}{2}x - 1\frac{1}{2}x$

4. $3c - (-5)c =$ _____

5. $5y - 3y + 11y =$ _____

6. $6g - 8g + 5g - 4g =$ _____

7. $n + n + n + n + n =$ _____

8. $n + 3n + 5n - 7n =$ _____

9. $2x + 4x - (-9)x =$ _____

10. $-7x + 2x + 3x =$ _____

Use with Lesson 9.3.

Combining Like Terms (cont.)

An expression like $2y + 6 + 4y - 8 - 9y + (-3)$ is difficult to work with because it is made up of six different terms that are added and subtracted.

There are two sets of like terms in the expression. The terms $2y$, $4y$, and $9y$ are like terms. The number terms in the expression—6, 8, and (-3)—are a second set of like terms. Each set of like terms can be combined into a single term. To simplify an expression that has more than one set of like terms, you must combine each set of like terms into a single term.

Example 3 Simplify $2y + 6 + 4y - 8 - 9y + (-3)$ by combining like terms.

Step 1 Combine the y terms. $2y + 4y - 9y = 6y - 9y = -3y$

Step 2 Combine the number terms. $6 - 8 + (-3) = -2 + (-3) = -5$

Final result: $2y + 6 + 4y - 8 - 9y + (-3) = -3y + (-5) = -3y - 5$

Check: Substitute 2 for y in both the original expression and the simplified expression.
$$2y + 6 + 4y - 8 - 9y + (-3) = -3y - 5$$
$$(2 * 2) + 6 + (4 * 2) - 8 - (9 * 2) + (-3) = (-3 * 2) - 5$$
$$4 + 6 + 8 - 8 - 18 + (-3) = -6 - 5$$
$$-11 = -11$$

Simplify each expression by combining like terms. Check each answer by substituting several values for the variable.

11. $4 + 7y + 20 =$ _____

12. $5x - 3x + 8 =$ _____

13. $5n + 6 - 8n - 2 - 3n =$ _____

14. $n + \pi + 2n - \frac{1}{2}\pi =$ _____

15. $-2.5x + 9 + 1.4x + 0.6 =$ _____

16. $9d + 2a - (-6a) + 3d - 15d =$ _____

Date _____   Time _____

Angle Measures

1. Use your protractor to measure the following angles.

    a.

    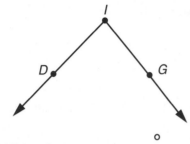

    ∠ DIG is about _____ °.

    b.

    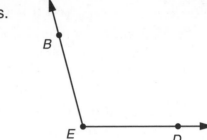

    ∠ BED is about _____ °.

    c.

    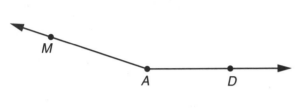

    ∠ MAD is about _____ °.

    d.

    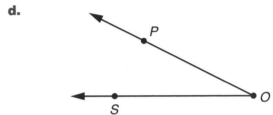

    ∠ SOP is about _____ °.

2. Find the measure of each angle in the polygons below. Write the measure inside the angle.

    a.

    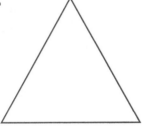

    b.

    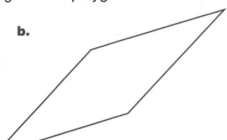

    c.

    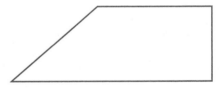

3. Draw a reflex angle. Label the vertex *A*.

    Measure the angle.   ∠A is about _____ °.

4. Draw an obtuse angle. Label the vertex *B*.

    Measure the angle.   ∠B is about _____ °.

5. Draw an acute angle. Label the vertex *C*.

    Measure the angle.   ∠C is about _____ °.

6. Draw and label a straight angle. Label the vertex *D*.

    The measure of a straight angle is _____ °.

Use with Lesson 9.3.

Simplifying Algebraic Expressions

Simplify the following expressions. First, use the distributive property to remove the parentheses. Then combine like terms. Check the answer by substituting a value for the variable.

Example Simplify $20 * (3 + 2x) + 30x$.

Step 1 Use the distributive property to remove the parentheses.

$$20 * (3 + 2x) + 30x = (20 * 3) + (20 * 2x) + 30x$$
$$= 60 + 40x + 30x$$
$$= 60 + 70x$$

Step 2 Simplify the expression by combining like terms.

Therefore,
Check by substituting 5 for x.

$$20 * (3 + 2x) + 30x = 60 + 70x$$
$$20 * (3 + 2 * 5) + 30 * 5 = 60 + 70 * 5$$
$$20 * (3 + 10) + 150 = 60 + 350$$
$$20 * 13 + 150 = 410$$
$$260 + 150 = 410$$
$$410 = 410$$

1. $7 + (5 - 3) * x + 1 = $ _____

2. $2(g - 1) + 1 - 5g = $ _____

3. $\frac{1}{2}(2m + 1) + \frac{1}{2} = $ _____

4. $n + 2n + 3n + (4 + 5)n + 6(7 + 2n) = $ _____

Challenge

5. $6(p - 7) - 5p + 15 + (3p + 2)4 = $ _____

Simplifying Equations

Simplify both sides of the following equations. Don't solve them.

Example $2b + 5 + 3b = 8 - b + 21$

$$(2b + 3b) + 5 = 8 - b + 21$$
$$5b + 5 = 8 - b + 21$$
$$5b + 5 = -b + 21 + 8$$
$$5b + 5 = -b + 29$$

1. $5h + 13h = 20 - 2$

2. $2 + x + 2x + 4 = x + 16$

3. $2(y + 2) = 4(y + 3)$

4. $(4 - 1)m - m = (m - 1) * 4$

5. $4y + 6 = 8(1 + y)$

6. $5(x + 3) - 2x = 35 + x$

7. $3 * (3.2 - 2c) = 4.6 + 4c$

8. $4(2z - 5) = z + 1$

Math Boxes 9.4

1. Frederick and Lucille conducted a survey to find out how many of their classmates had brothers and sisters. They surveyed 31 students and learned that 18 had at least one sister and 21 had at least one brother.

   Draw a Venn diagram to represent the results of Frederick and Lucille's survey.

   How many students had at least one brother and one sister? _____

2. Write >, <, or =.

   a. $12 - (-3)$ _____ $\frac{7}{8} \div \frac{1}{20}$

   b. $5^2 + 3^2$ _____ $5\frac{20}{3} + 10\frac{50}{10}$

   c. $3\frac{6}{7} + 2\frac{3}{5}$ _____ $\frac{100}{18}$

   d. $0.48 * 2.5$ _____ $3 * 0.26$

   e. $-7 * -6$ _____ $-7 * 6$

3. Larry was reading a biography of Abraham Lincoln. He read 30 pages in 40 minutes.

   a. How many pages did he read in 60 minutes?

   _____

   b. Write a proportion to solve the problem.

   _____

4. Multiply. Write each answer in simplest form.

   a. $4\frac{3}{7} * \frac{6}{5} =$ _____

   b. $\frac{16}{11} * 4\frac{2}{3} =$ _____

   c. $\frac{25}{4} * \frac{10}{6} =$ _____

   d. $3\frac{1}{7} * 5\frac{8}{9} =$ _____

   e. $7 * \frac{6}{15} =$ _____

5. Complete.

   a. _____ $= 80\%$ of 80

   b. _____ $= 75\%$ of 128

   c. _____ $= 66\frac{2}{3}\%$ of 189

   d. 60% of $255 =$ _____

   e. 37.5% of $480 =$ _____

Simplifying and Solving Equations

Simplify each equation. Then solve it. Record the operations you used for each step.

1. $6y - 2y = 40$

Solution _____

2. $5p + 28 = 88 - p$

Solution _____

3. $8d - 3d = 65$

Solution _____

4. $12e - 19 = 7 - e$

Solution _____

5. $3n + \frac{1}{2}n = 42$

Solution _____

6. $3m - 1 + m + 6 = 2 - 9$

Solution _____

7. $3(1 + 2y) = y + 2y + 4y$

Solution _____

8. $8 - 12x = 6 * (1 + x)$

Solution _____

9. $-4.8 + b + 0.6b = 1.8 + 3.6b$

Solution _____

10. $4t - 5 = t + 7$

Solution _____

Use with Lesson 9.5.

Simplifying and Solving Equations (cont.)

11. $8v - 25 = v + 80$

12. $3z + 6z = 60 - z$

Solution _____

Solution _____

13. $g + 3g + 32 = 27 + 5g + 2$

14. $16 + 3s - 2s = 24 + 2s - 20$

Solution _____

Solution _____

15. Are the following two equations equivalent? _____

$5y + 3 = -6y + 4 + 12y$ $5y + 3 = -6y + 4(1 + 3y)$

Explain your answer. _____

_____

_____

16. Are the following two equations equivalent? _____

$5(f - 2) + 6 = 16$ $f - 1 = 3$

Explain your answer. _____

_____

_____

Challenge

17. Solve $\dfrac{2z + 4}{5} = z - 1$ _____

(*Hint:* Multiply both sides by 5.)

Number Stories and the Distributive Property

Solve the problems in your head. Do not use a calculator. For each problem, record the number model you used.

1. A carton of milk costs $0.60. John bought 3 cartons of milk one day and 4 cartons the next day.

How much did he spend in all? _____

Number model _____

2. During a typical week, Karen runs 16 miles, and Jacob runs 14 miles.

About how many miles in all do Karen and Jacob run in 8 weeks? _____

Number model _____

3. Mark bought 6 CDs that cost $12 each. He returned 2 of them.

How much did he spend in all? _____

Number model _____

4. Max collects stamps. He had 9 envelopes, each containing 25 stamps. He sold 3 envelopes to another collector.

How many stamps did he have left? _____

Number model _____

5. Jean is sending party invitations to her friends. She has 8 boxes with 12 invitations in each box. She has already mailed 5 boxes of invitations.

How many invitations are left? _____

Number model _____

Use with Lesson 9.5.

Math Boxes 9.5

---

1. Measure the angles.

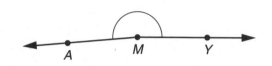

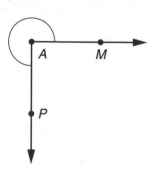

    a. Reflex ∠*AMY* measures about

    _____ °.

    b. Reflex ∠*PAM* measures about

    _____ °.

---

2. Multiply.

$254 * 38 =$ _____

3. Divide.

    a. $\frac{4}{5} \div \frac{2}{7} =$ _____

    b. $\frac{1}{9} \div \frac{5}{6} =$ _____

    c. $\frac{2}{3} \div \frac{10}{7} =$ _____

    d. _____ $= \frac{4}{9} \div \frac{8}{5}$

    e. _____ $= 8 \div \frac{8}{7}$

---

4. Circle the equation that describes the relationship between the numbers in the table.

$4y = \frac{1}{4} + x$

$4x + 12 = y$

$y = 0.4 + x$

$x = 4y + 0.4$

x	y
2	20
5	32
$\frac{1}{2}$	14
0.1	12.4

5. Evaluate each expression. Use the rules for order of operations.

    a. $6 + 9 \div (-3) =$ _____

    b. $15 + 2^2 - 8 \div 4 =$ _____

    c. $9 * (6 + 2) - (-5) =$ _____

    d. $7 + 3 * 4 + (-8) =$ _____

    e. $(8 + 3) * -4 =$ _____

Date _____   Time _____

Mobile Problems

The mobile shown in each problem is in balance.
The **fulcrum** is the center point of the rod.
A mobile will balance if $W * D = w * d$.

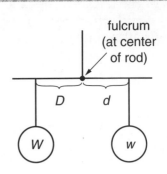

Write and solve an equation to answer each question.

1. What is the distance from the fulcrum to the object on the right of the fulcrum?

$W =$ _____ $D =$ _____ $w =$ _____ $d =$ _____

Equation _____   Solution _____

Distance _____ units

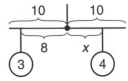

2. What is the weight of the object on the left of the fulcrum?

$W =$ _____ $D =$ _____ $w =$ _____ $d =$ _____

Equation _____   Solution _____

Weight _____ units

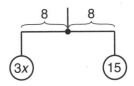

3. What is the distance from the fulcrum to each of the objects?

$W =$ _____ $D =$ _____ $w =$ _____ $d =$ _____

Equation _____   Solution _____

Distance on the left of the fulcrum _____ units

Distance on the right of the fulcrum _____ units

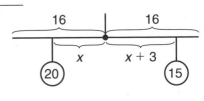

4. What is the weight of each object?

$W =$ _____ $D =$ _____ $w =$ _____ $d =$ _____

Equation _____   Solution _____

Weight of the object on the left of the fulcrum _____ units

Weight of the object on the right of the fulcrum _____ units

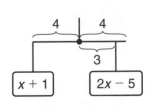

Use with Lesson 9.6.

Partial-Quotients Division

Use the partial-quotients division algorithm to find quotients correct
to two decimal places. Show your work on the computation grid.

1. $\dfrac{1{,}285}{7}$ _____

2. $3{,}709 \div 18$ _____

3. $42\overline{)7{,}956}$ _____

4. $\dfrac{282.25}{16}$ _____

5. $19.015 \div 38$ _____

6. $3.8\overline{)746.85}$ _____

Math Boxes 9.6

---

1. Find a kite on your Geometry Template. Use the template to draw a kite in the space to the right.

How would you describe a kite?

_____

_____

_____

_____

SRB
156 157

---

2. Solve.

Solution

a. $\frac{15}{2} = \frac{y}{6}$ _____

b. $\frac{x}{99} = \frac{10}{11}$ _____

c. $\frac{144}{3} = \frac{x}{1}$ _____

d. $\frac{24}{x} = \frac{80}{100}$ _____

e. $\frac{50}{x} = \frac{18}{72}$ _____

SRB
111–113

3. Seven out of nine cards are faceup. If 16 cards are facedown, how many cards are there altogether?

_____

Explain how you found your answer.

_____

_____

_____

_____

SRB
116–118

---

4. The table at the right shows how much a person weighing 100 pounds on Earth would weigh on each of the planets in the solar system.

a. On which planet would a person weigh about $\frac{1}{6}$ as much as on Mercury? _____

b. On which planet would a person weigh about 3 times as much as on Mars?

_____

c. On which planet would a person weigh about $2\frac{1}{2}$ times as much as on Earth?

_____

Planet	Weight (lb)
Mercury	37
Venus	88
Earth	100
Mars	38
Jupiter	264
Saturn	115
Uranus	93
Neptune	122
Pluto	6

SRB
239

A Picnic Budget Spreadsheet

The following spreadsheet gives budget information for a class picnic.

	A	B	C	D
		Class Picnic ($)		
1		budget for class picnic		
2				
3	quantity	food items	unit price	cost
4	6	packages of hamburgers	2.79	16.74
5	5	packages of hamburger buns	1.29	6.45
6	3	bags of potato chips	3.12	9.36
7	3	quarts of macaroni salad	4.50	13.50
8	4	bottles of soft drinks	1.69	6.76
9			subtotal	52.81
10			8% tax	4.23
11			total	57.04

1. What information is shown in Row 8? _____

2. What kind of information is shown in
   Column A (labels, numbers, or formulas)? _____

3. Cell D6 holds the formula D6 = A6 * C6.

   a. What formula is stored in Cell D4? _____

   b. What formula is stored in Cell D8? _____

4. Circle the formula stored in Cell D9.

   D9 = C4 + C5 + C6 + C7 + C8   D9 = D4 + D5 + D6 + D7 + D8

5. a. What is calculated by the formula stored in Cell D10? _____

   b. Circle the formula stored in Cell D10.

      D10 = 0.08 * C9   D10 = 0.08 * D9   D10 = 8 * D9

6. a. What is calculated by the formula stored in Cell D11? _____

   b. Write the formula stored in D11. _____

7. a. Which cells in the spreadsheet would change if you
      changed the number of bags of potato chips to 4? _____

   b. Calculate the number that would be shown in each of these cells.

   _____

Shading Ratios

Use the design at the right to answer Problems 1–3.

1. What is the ratio of unshaded squares to shaded squares? _____

2. What is the ratio of shaded squares to total squares? _____

3. Describe in words the ratio of unshaded squares to total squares. _____

_____

Use the design at the right to answer Problems 4–7.

4. Write two ratios that describe the design.

_____

_____

_____

5. Shade more triangles so that the resulting ratio of shaded to total is 2 out of 3.

6. How many triangles did you have to shade? _____

7. Explain what a ratio of 1:2 might describe in the design *after* you shaded triangles in Problem 5.

_____

_____

Use with Lesson 9.7.

1. Fill in each shape so that it becomes a recognizable figure. See the example at the right.

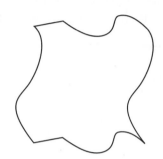

a.

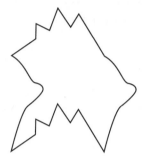

b.

2. a. Use a compass to draw two concentric circles. The radius of the smaller circle is 1.5 centimeters. The radius of the larger circle is 2 centimeters.

b. What is the area of the ring between the two circles? Use the π key on a calculator, or 3.14, as the value for π.

_____

SRB
200

3. Without using a protractor, find the measure of each numbered angle. Write each measure on the drawing.

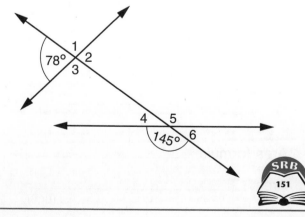

SRB
151

4. Add or subtract. Do not use a calculator. Write your answers in simplest form.

a. _____ $= \frac{2}{3} + 7\frac{4}{5}$

b. _____ $= 12\frac{2}{7} + \frac{3}{8}$

c. _____ $= 7\frac{2}{5} - \frac{29}{4}$

d. _____ $= \frac{9}{15} - 1\frac{4}{5}$

e. _____ $= 4\frac{2}{8} + 7\frac{3}{11}$

SRB
80 81
93

Area Formulas

Calculate the area of each figure below. A summary of useful area formulas appears on pages 197–200 of the *Student Reference Book.*

Measure any dimensions you need to the nearest tenth of a centimeter. Record the dimensions next to each figure. You may need to draw and measure one or two line segments on a figure. Round your answers to the nearest square centimeter.

1.

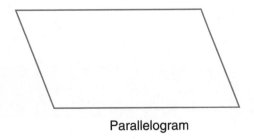

Circle

Area formula _____

Area _____
                        (unit)

2.

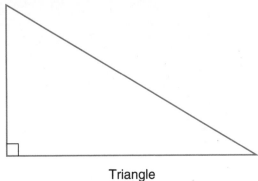

Triangle

Area formula _____

Area _____
                        (unit)

3.

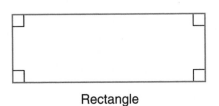

Rectangle

Area formula _____

Area _____
                        (unit)

4.

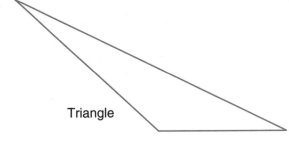

Triangle

Area formula _____

Area _____
                        (unit)

5.

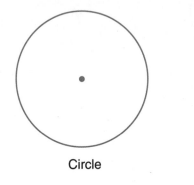

Parallelogram

Area formula _____

Area _____
                        (unit)

6. Challenge

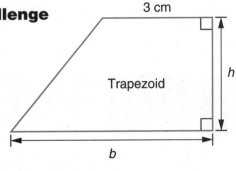

Trapezoid

Area formula _____

Area _____
                        (unit)

Use with Lesson 9.8.

Math Boxes 9.8

1. Find a rhombus on your Geometry Template. Use the template to draw a rhombus in the space below.

How would you describe a rhombus?

_____

_____

_____

_____

2. Solve.

Solution

a. $24 * f = 12$ _____

b. $\frac{y}{15} = 3$ _____

c. $n - 136 = 65$ _____

d. $\frac{36}{q} = 3$ _____

e. $\frac{2{,}000}{y} = 50$ _____

3. The ratio of facedown to faceup cards is 5:4. If there are 72 cards altogether, how many cards are faceup?

_____

Explain how you found your answer.

_____

_____

_____

_____

_____

4. The table at the right shows how many calories per hour a person weighing 150 pounds uses for various activities.

a. For which activity does the person use about $\frac{1}{6}$ of the number of calories used in running?

_____

b. For which activity does the person use about 2.5 times as many calories as when sleeping?

_____

c. For which activity does the person use about $\frac{2}{3}$ of the number of calories used in walking?

_____

Activity	Calories Per Hour
Sleeping	60
Sitting	100
Standing	140
Driving	150
Walking	225
Volleyball	350
Basketball	500
Running	600

Perimeter, Circumference, and Area

Solve each problem. Explain your answers.

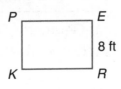

1. Rectangle *PERK* has a perimeter of 40 feet.

   Length of side *PE* _____
   (unit)

   Area of Rectangle *PERK* _____
   (unit)

_____

_____

_____

_____

2. The area of Triangle *ABC* is 300 meters².
   What is the length of side *AB*?

   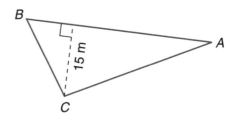

   Length of side *AB* _____
   (unit)

_____

_____

_____

_____

3. The area of Parallelogram *KLMN* is 72 square inches.

   The length of side *LX* is 6 inches, and the
   length of side *KY* is 3 inches.

   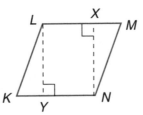

   What is the length of $\overline{LY}$?

   Length of $\overline{LY}$ _____
   (unit)

_____

_____

_____

_____

Use with Lesson 9.8.

Perimeter, Circumference, and Area (cont.)

4. The area of Triangle *ACE* is 42 square yards.
What is the area of Rectangle *BCDE*?

Area of Rectangle *BCDE* _____

_____

_____

_____

_____

_____

_____

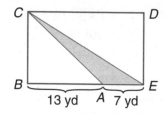

5. To the nearest percent, about what percent of the area
of the square is covered by the area of the circle?

Answer _____

_____

_____

_____

_____

_____

_____

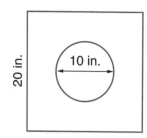

6. Which path is longer: once around the figure 8—from *A,* to *B,*
to *C,* to *B,* and back to *A*—or once around the large circle?

_____

_____

_____

_____

_____

_____

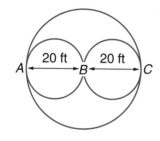

Calculating the Volume of the Human Body

An average adult human male is about 69 inches (175 centimeters) tall and weighs about 170 pounds (77 kilograms). The drawings below show how a man's body may be approximated by 7 cylinders, 1 rectangular prism, and 1 sphere.

The drawings use the scale 1 mm:1 cm. This means that every length of 1 millimeter in the drawing represents 1 centimeter of actual body length. The drawing below is 175 millimeters high. Therefore, it represents a male who is 175 centimeters tall.

head
(sphere)

neck
(cylinder)

torso
(rectangular
prism)

2 arms
(cylinders)

2 upper legs
(cylinders)

2 lower legs
(cylinders)

scale is 1 mm:1 cm

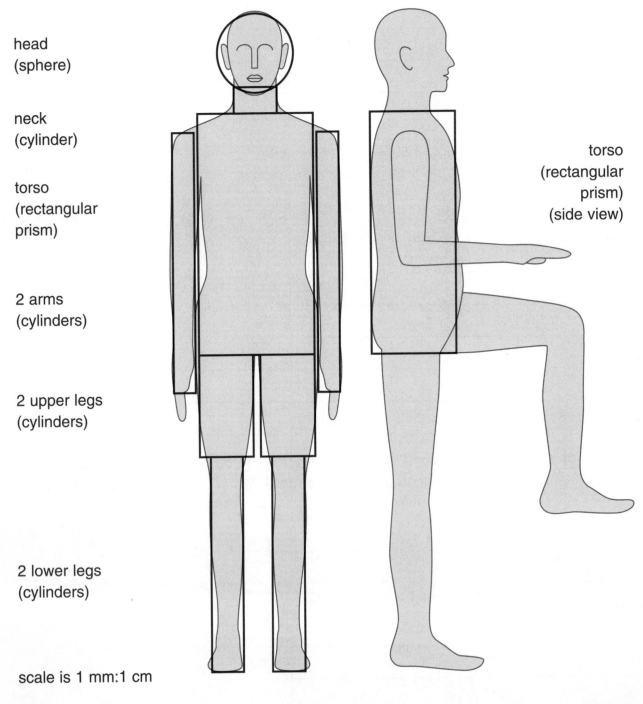

torso
(rectangular
prism)
(side view)

Use with Lesson 9.9.

Calculating the Volume of the Human Body (cont.)

1. **a.** Use a centimeter ruler to estimate the diameters of the cylinders and sphere and the dimensions of the rectangular prism shown on page 366. Record your estimates on the drawing. Then record the radius of each cylinder and the sphere and the dimensions of the rectangular prism in the table below. (To find the radius, divide the diameter by 2.) Be sure to record the actual body dimensions. For example, if you measure the length of an arm as 72 millimeters, record this as 72 centimeters, because the scale of the drawings is 1 mm:1 cm.

   b. Calculate the volume of each body part and record it in the table. You will find a summary of useful volume formulas on pages 203, 204, and 206 in your *Student Reference Book*.

   For the arm, upper leg, and lower leg, multiply the volume by 2. Add to find the total volume of an average adult male's body. Your answer will be in cubic centimeters.

Body Part and Shape	Actual Body Dimensions (cm)		Volume (Round to the nearest 1,000 cm³.)
head (sphere)	radius:		* 1 =
neck (cylinder)	radius:	height:	* 1 =
torso (rectangular prism)	length: height:	width:	* 1 =
arm (cylinder)	radius:	height:	* 2 =
upper leg (cylinder)	radius:	height:	* 2 =
lower leg (cylinder)	radius:	height:	* 2 =
		Total Volume:	About

2. One liter is equal to 1,000 cubic centimeters. Use this fact to complete the following statement: I estimate that the total volume of an average adult male's body is about _____ liters.

3. John weighs about 136 pounds. What is the ratio of John's weight to the average adult male's weight of about 170 pounds?   Ratio _____ to 1

   Use the ratio to estimate the volume of John's body.

   The volume of John's body is about _____ cm³, or about _____ liters.

Data Review

1. Below are the scores for a spelling test in Ms. Jenning's sixth grade class:

72%	96%	88%	96%	80%	68%	44%
76%	96%	68%	56%	76%	96%	92%
80%	88%	68%	56%	100%	100%	88%
68%	96%	92%	96%	76%	80%	88%

   a. Make a stem-and-leaf plot of these data.

   b. Find the following landmarks:

   maximum _____   median _____

   mode _____

2. The First Bank and Trust raised the interest rate on savings accounts four times in one year. To the right is a graph of the interest rates for the year. Use the graph to answer the questions.

   **Interest Rates at
   The First Bank and Trust**

   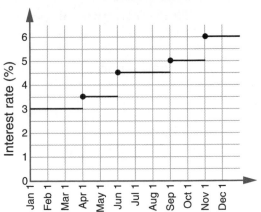

   a. What was the interest rate in July? _____

   b. How long did the
   interest rate stay at 4.5%? _____

   c. How much did the interest rate
   increase from February to October? _____

3. Match each mystery graph with its most likely title from the list below.

   Graph _____   Graph _____   Graph _____

   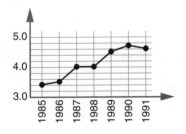   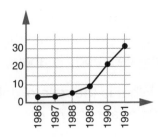   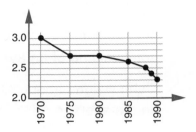

   A   Number of Cellular Phones (hundred-thousands)
   B   Egg Consumption Per Person (hundreds)
   C   Total Amount Paid in Personal Income Tax (hundred-billions)

                                                       Use with Lesson 9.9.

Math Boxes 9.9

---

1. Fill in each shape so that it becomes a recognizable figure. See the example at the right.

a.

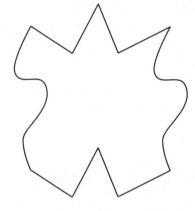

b.

---

2. a. Use a compass to draw a circle whose circumference is about 15.7 centimeters. Use the π key on a calculator or 3.14 as the value for π.

  b. Describe what you did to solve the problem.

  _____

  _____

  _____

---

3. Without using a protractor, find the measure of each numbered angle. Write each measure on the drawing. Lines *a* and *b* are parallel.

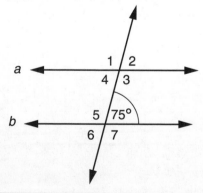

4. Add or subtract. Do not use a calculator. Write your answers in simplest form.

  a. _____ $= \frac{3}{4} + 5\frac{5}{6}$

  b. _____ $= 12 - (-2\frac{2}{3})$

  c. _____ $= 15\frac{4}{5} - 20$

  d. _____ $= 7\frac{11}{12} + \frac{25}{4}$

  e. _____ $= 9\frac{3}{8} - 5\frac{3}{4}$

Solving Equations by Trial and Error

If you substitute a number for the variable in an equation and the result is a true number sentence, then that number is a solution of the equation. One way to solve an equation is to try several **test numbers** until you find the solution. Each test number can help you "close in" on the exact solution. Using this **trial-and-error method** for solving equations, you may not find the exact solution, but you can come very close to the exact solution.

Example Find a solution of the equation $\frac{1}{x} + x = 4$ by trial and error. If you can't find an exact solution, try to find a number that is very close to an exact solution.

The table shows the results of substituting several test numbers for x.

x	$\frac{1}{x}$	$\frac{1}{x} + x$	Compare ($\frac{1}{x} + x$) to 4
1	1	2	less than 4
2	0.5	2.5	still less than 4, but closer
3	0.3	3.3	less than 4, but even closer
4	0.25	4.25	greater than 4

These results suggest that we try testing numbers for x that are between 3 and 4.

x	$\frac{1}{x}$	$\frac{1}{x} + x$	Compare ($\frac{1}{x} + x$) to 4
3.9	0.256…	4.156…	>4
3.6	$0.2\overline{7}$	$3.8\overline{7}$	<4

We're getting closer. Now it's your turn. Try other test numbers. See how close you can get to 4 for the value of $\frac{1}{x} + x$.

x	$\frac{1}{x}$	$\frac{1}{x} + x$	Compare ($\frac{1}{x} + x$) to 4

My closest solution _____

     Use with Lesson 9.10.

Solving Equations by Trial and Error (cont.)

Find the numbers that are closest to the solutions of the equations.
Use the suggested test numbers to get started.

1. Equation: $\sqrt{y} + y = 10$

y	$\sqrt{y}$	$\sqrt{y} + y$	Compare $(\sqrt{y} + y)$ to 10
0	0	0	<10
5	2.24	7.24	
9	3		

My closest solution _____

2. Equation: $x^2 - 3x = 8$

x	x^2	$3x$	$x^2 - 3x$	Compare $(x^2 - 3x)$ to 8
4				
6				
5				

My closest solution _____

Formulas, Tables, and Graphs

For each problem, use the formula to complete the table. Graph the number pairs from the table. Then connect the points you plot to make a line graph.

1. *Formula:* $y = (-2) * x$

x	y
0	
1	
	−6
−1	
	6

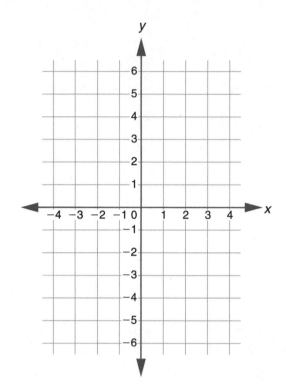

2. *Formula:* $D = 2t - 3$

t	D
0	
1	
	3
−1	
	−7

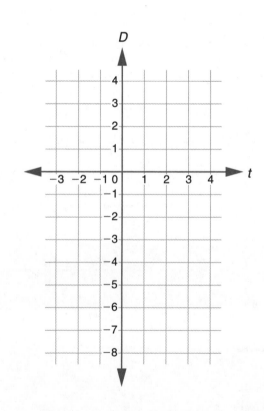

                                               Use with Lesson 9.10.

Math Boxes 9.10

1. Draw the line(s) of symmetry for each figure below.

SRB
170

2. Use quick common denominators to decide which fraction is larger. Circle the larger one.

a. $\frac{6}{27}$ $\frac{1}{5}$

b. $\frac{4}{7}$ $\frac{27}{53}$

c. $\frac{9}{11}$ $\frac{74}{91}$

d. $\frac{19}{5}$ $\frac{46}{12}$

e. $\frac{8}{26}$ $\frac{5}{12}$

SRB
73

3. Multiply or divide.

a. $-150 / 15 =$ _____

b. $-16 * (-4) =$ _____

c. $20 * (-9) =$ _____

d. $-180 / 30 =$ _____

e. $360 / (-4) =$ _____

SRB
95

4. Use the distributive property. Show your work.

a. $7 * (30 - 3) =$ _____

_____

_____

b. $12 * (10 + 5) =$ _____

_____

_____

SRB
230 231

5. Follow the directions for the coordinate grid.

a. Mark point $(4, -2)$. Label it *A*.

b. Mark point $(-4, 2)$. Label it *B*.

c. Draw line segment *AB*.

d. Find the coordinates of the midpoint of $\overline{AB}$. (_____ , _____)

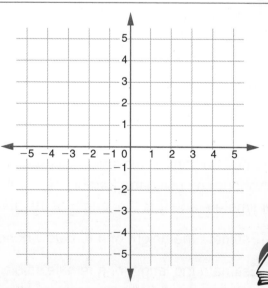

SRB
216

Using Formulas to Solve Problems

To solve a problem using a formula, you can substitute the known quantities for variables in the formula and solve the resulting equation.

Example A formula for converting between Celsius and Fahrenheit temperatures is $F = 1.8C + 32$, where C represents the Celsius temperature and F the Fahrenheit temperature.

- Use the formula to convert 30°C to degrees Fahrenheit.

	$F = 1.8C + 32$
Substitute 30 for C in the formula:	$F = (1.8 * 30) + 32$
Solve the equation:	$F = 86$
Answer:	30°C $= 86$°F

- Use the formula to convert 50°F to degrees Celsius.

	$F = 1.8C + 32$
Substitute 50 for F in the formula:	$50 = (1.8 * C) + 32$
Solve the equation:	$10 = C$
Answer:	50°F $= 10$°C

1. The formula $W = 570A - 850$ expresses the relationship between the average number of words small children know and their ages (for ages 2 to 8). The variable W represents the number of words known, and A represents the age in years.

   a. About how many words might a $3\frac{1}{4}$-year-old child know? _____

   b. About how old might a child be who knows about 1,700 words? _____

2. A bowler whose average score is less than 200 is given a handicap. The **handicap** is a number of points that is added to a bowler's score for each game. A common handicap formula is $H = 0.8 * (200 - A)$, where H is the handicap and A is the average score.

   a. What is the handicap of a bowler whose average score is 160? _____

   b. What is the average score of a bowler whose handicap is 68? _____

3. An adult human female's height can be estimated from the length of her tibia (shinbone) by using the formula $H = 2.4 * T + 75$, where H is the height in centimeters and T is the length of the tibia in centimeters.

   a. Estimate the height of a female whose tibia is 31 centimeters long. _____

   b. Estimate the length of a female's tibia if she is 175 centimeters tall. _____

Use with Lesson 9.11.

Date _____   Time _____

Volume Problems

Solve each problem. You may need to look up formulas in your
Student Reference Book. Check your answers.

1. The capacity (volume) of the desk drawer is 1,365 in.^{3}.
Find the depth (d) of the drawer.

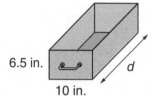

6.5 in.

10 in.

d

Formula _____

Substitute _____

Solve _____

_____

Depth of drawer = _____

2. The cylindrical can has a capacity of 4 liters (4 liters = 4,000 cm^3).
Find the height (h) of the can, to the nearest centimeter.

8 cm

h

Formula _____

Substitute _____

Solve _____

_____

Height is about _____.

3. A soccer ball has a 9-inch diameter.

9 in.

   a. What is the shape of the
   smallest box that will hold the ball? _____

   b. What are the dimensions of the box? _____

   c. Compare the volume of the box to the volume of the ball. Is the
   volume of the box more or less than twice the volume of the ball? _____
   (*Reminder:* A formula for finding the volume of a sphere is $V = \frac{4}{3} * \pi * r^3$.)

   Explain your answer. _____

   _____

   _____

   _____

Date _____   Time _____

Angle, Perimeter, and Area Problems

Solve each problem. Check your answers.

1. $\angle ABC$ is a right angle. What is the degree measure of $\angle CBD$? Of $\angle ABD$?

   Equation _____

   Solve.

   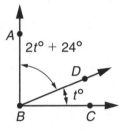

   Measure of $\angle CBD$ = _____ °   Measure of $\angle ABD$ = _____ °

2. Triangle *MJQ* and Square *EFGH* have the same perimeter. The dimensions are given in millimeters. What are the lengths of sides *MQ* and *MJ* in Triangle *MJQ*?

   Equation _____

   Solve.

   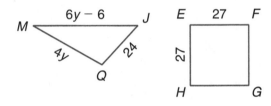

   Length of $\overline{MQ}$ = _____   Length of $\overline{MJ}$ = _____

3. The area of the shaded part of Rectangle *RSTU* is 78 ft². Find the length of side *TU*.

   Equation _____

   Solve.

   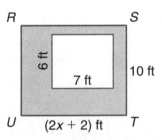

   Length of side *TU* = _____

1. Circle all the regular polygons.

Explain why the circled figures are regular polygons.

_____

_____

_____

_____

SRB 152 153

2. Solve.

Solution

a. $\frac{22}{m} = \frac{1}{2}$ _____

b. $0.25 * s = 64$ _____

c. $d * 10^2 = 420.5$ _____

d. $f * \frac{1}{8} = \frac{3}{16}$ _____

e. $\sqrt{h} = 20$ _____

SRB 233 234

---

3. When Marlene removed her dinner from the freezer, the temperature of the dinner was −10°C. She heated the dinner in the oven, and then put it on the table. It cooled to room temperature, 23°C, while she was talking on the phone.

How many degrees warmer was the dinner at room temperature than it was when removed from the freezer? _____

Write a number model to show how you found your answer.

_____

SRB 225

---

4. The table shows the results of a survey that asked people where they keep their computers at home. Fill in the missing information in the table. Use a protractor to make a circle graph of the results. Do not use the Percent Circle.

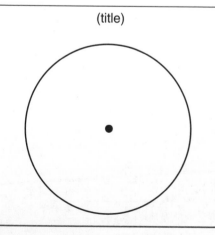

_____
(title)

Location	Number of People	Percent of Total
Family room	20	
Bedroom	10	
Living room	8	
Home office	8	
Kitchen	2	
Basement	2	
Total		

SRB 141

Squares and Square Roots of Numbers

Math Message

You know that the **square of a number** is equal to the number multiplied by itself. For example, $5^2 = 5 * 5 = 25$.

The **square root** of a number *n* is a number whose square is *n*. For example, a square root of 25 is 5, because $5^2 = 5 * 5 = 25$. The square root of 25 is also equal to -5, because $(-5) * (-5) = (-5)^2 = 25$. So every positive number has two square roots, which are opposites of each other.

We use the symbol $\sqrt{}$ to write positive square roots. $\sqrt{25}$ is read as *the positive square root of 25.*

1. Write the square root of each number.

   a. $\sqrt{81} =$ _____   **b.** $\sqrt{100} =$ _____   **c.** $\sqrt{100^2} =$ _____

2. What is the square root of zero? _____

3. Can a negative number have a square root? _____

   Explain. _____

   _____

   _____

To find the positive square root of a number with a calculator, use the  key. For example, to find the square root of 25, enter $\sqrt{}$ 25 $)$ Enter . The display will show 5.

4. Use a calculator. Round your answers for a. and d. to the nearest hundredth.

   a. $\sqrt{17} =$ _____   **b.** $\sqrt{17} * \sqrt{17} =$ _____   **c.** $\sqrt{\pi} * \sqrt{\pi} =$ _____

   d. $\sqrt{\pi} =$ _____   **e.** $\left(\sqrt{17}\right)^2 =$ _____   **f.** $\sqrt{\frac{1}{16}} =$ _____

5. The length of a side of a square is $\sqrt{6.25}$ centimeters.
   What is the area of the square?   _____

6. The area of a square is 21 square inches.
   What is the length of a side, to the nearest tenth of an inch?   _____

7. The radius of a circle is $\sqrt{20}$ feet.
   What is its area, to the nearest hundredth?   About _____

Verifying the Pythagorean Theorem

In a right triangle, the side opposite the right angle is called the **hypotenuse.** The other two sides are called the **legs of the triangle.**

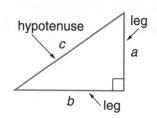

Think about the following statement:
If a and b are the lengths of the legs of a right triangle and c is the length of the hypotenuse, then $a^2 + b^2 = c^2$.

This statement is known as the **Pythagorean Theorem.**

1. To verify that the Pythagorean Theorem is true, use a blank sheet of paper that has square corners. Draw diagonal lines to form 4 right triangles, one at each corner. Then measure the lengths of the legs and the hypotenuse of each right triangle, to the nearest millimeter. Record the lengths in the table below. Then complete the table.

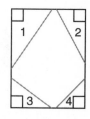

Triangle	Leg (a)	Leg (b)	Hypotenuse (c)	$a^2 + b^2$	c^2
1					
2					
3					
4					

2. Compare $(a^2 + b^2)$ to c^2 for each of the triangles you drew.
   Why might these two numbers be slightly different?

   _____

   _____

   _____

3. Use the Pythagorean Theorem to find c^2 for the triangle at the right.
   Then find the length c.

   $c^2 =$ _____ c is about _____ .

Using the Pythagorean Theorem

In Problems 1–6, use the Pythagorean Theorem to find each missing length.
Round your answer to the nearest tenth.

1.

Equation $\underline{\quad c^2 = 5^2 + 12^2 \quad}$

$c^2 = \underline{\quad\quad}$ $c = \underline{\quad\quad}$

2.

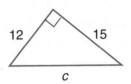

Equation $\underline{\quad\quad\quad\quad\quad}$

$c^2 = \underline{\quad\quad}$ $c = \underline{\quad\quad}$

3.

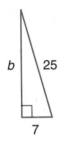

Equation $\underline{\quad\quad\quad\quad\quad}$

$b^2 = \underline{\quad\quad}$ $b = \underline{\quad\quad}$

4.

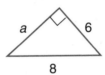

Equation $\underline{\quad\quad\quad\quad\quad}$

$a^2 = \underline{\quad\quad}$ $a = \underline{\quad\quad}$

5.

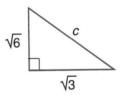

Equation $\underline{\quad\quad\quad\quad\quad}$

$c^2 = \underline{\quad\quad}$ $c = \underline{\quad\quad}$

6.

Equation $\underline{\quad\quad\quad\quad\quad}$

$s^2 = \underline{\quad\quad}$ $s = \underline{\quad\quad}$

7. Is the triangle shown at the right a right triangle? $\underline{\quad\quad}$

Explain. $\underline{\quad\quad\quad\quad\quad\quad\quad\quad\quad\quad\quad\quad}$

$\underline{\quad\quad\quad\quad\quad\quad\quad\quad\quad\quad\quad\quad\quad\quad\quad\quad\quad\quad}$

$\underline{\quad\quad\quad\quad\quad\quad\quad\quad\quad\quad\quad\quad\quad\quad\quad\quad\quad\quad}$

$\underline{\quad\quad\quad\quad\quad\quad\quad\quad\quad\quad\quad\quad\quad\quad\quad\quad\quad\quad}$

                                                        Use with Lesson 9.12.

Math Boxes 9.12

1. Draw the line(s) of symmetry for each figure below.

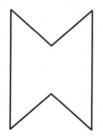 

2. Use quick common denominators to decide which fraction is larger. Circle the larger one.

a. $\frac{2}{15}$ $\frac{5}{31}$

b. $\frac{8}{41}$ $\frac{5}{22}$

c. $\frac{3}{62}$ $\frac{4}{75}$

d. $\frac{12}{39}$ $\frac{7}{19}$

e. $\frac{3}{16}$ $\frac{1}{6}$

3. Multiply or divide.

a. $-25 * 8 =$ _____

b. $-280 / -70 =$ _____

c. $-40 * -90 =$ _____

d. $540 \div (-6) =$ _____

e. $80 * -300 =$ _____

4. Use the distributive property. Show your work.

a. $5 * (25 + 40) =$ _____

_____

_____

b. $11 * (50 - 3) =$ _____

_____

_____

5. Follow the directions for the coordinate grid.

a. Mark point $(-4,3)$. Label it *M*.

b. Mark point $(5,3)$. Label it *A*.

c. Mark point $(4,-1)$. Label it *T*.

d. Mark point *H* so that the polygon *MATH* is a parallelogram. Draw parallelogram *MATH*.

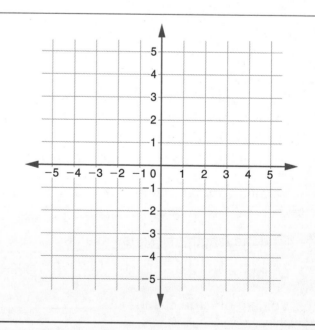

Similar Figures and the Size-Change Factor

The two butterfly clamps shown below are similar because they each have the same shape. One clamp is an enlargement of the other. The size-change factor tells the amount of enlargement.

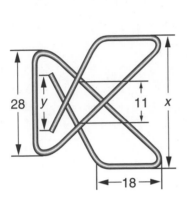 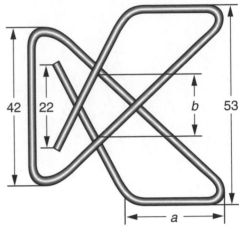

unit: millimeters (mm)

1. The size-change factor for the clamps shown above is _____.

In Problems 2–5, use the size-change factor to find the missing lengths.

2. $a =$ _____ mm = _____ cm

3. $b =$ _____ mm = _____ cm

4. $x =$ _____ mm = _____ cm

5. $y =$ _____ mm = _____ cm

6. If a butterfly clamp is straightened out, it forms a long, thin cylinder. When the small clamp is straightened out, it is 21 cm long, and the thickness (diameter) of the clamp is 0.15 cm. Its radius is 0.075 cm. Calculate the volume of the small clamp. Use the formula $V = \pi r^2 h$.

 Volume of small clamp = _____ cm^3 (to the nearest thousandth cm^3)

7. Find the length, thickness (diameter), and volume of the large clamp.

 Length = _____ cm   Diameter = _____ cm

 Volume of large clamp = _____ cm^3 (to the nearest thousandth cm^3)

Use with Lesson 9.13.

Date _____   Time _____

Indirect Measurement Problems

In the problems that follow, you are going to use **indirect methods** to determine the heights and lengths of objects that you cannot measure directly.

1. A tree is too tall to measure, but it casts a shadow that is 18 feet long. Ike is standing near the tree. He is 5 feet tall and casts a shadow that is 6 feet long.

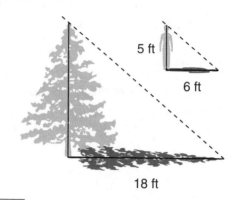

   The light rays, the tree, and its shadow form a triangle that is **similar** to the triangle formed by the light rays, Ike, and his shadow.

   What is the size-change factor of the triangles? _____

   About how tall is the tree? _____

2. Ike's dad is 6 feet tall. He is standing near the Washington Monument, which is 555 feet tall. Ike's dad casts a 7-foot shadow. About how long a shadow does the Washington Monument cast? (*Hint:* Draw sketches that include the above information.) _____

Challenge

3. A surveyor wants to find the distance between points *A* and *B* on opposite ends of a lake. He sets a stake at point *C* so that angle *ABC* is a right angle. By measuring, he finds that $\overline{AC}$ is 95 meters long and $\overline{BC}$ is 76 meters long.

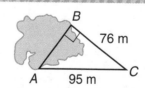

   How far across the lake is it from point *A* to point *B*? _____

Math Boxes 9.13

---

1. I am a regular polygon with all obtuse angles. I have the smallest number of sides of any polygon with obtuse angles. How many sides do I have?

_____

Use your Geometry Template to draw me below.

2. Solve.

Solution

a. $w * 10^{-2} = 28.2$ _____

b. $420 * k = 140$ _____

c. $\frac{5}{2} - p = \frac{7}{4}$ _____

d. $18 / a = -6$ _____

e. $2^d = 64$ _____

---

3. The high temperature in Chicago on January 3 was 38°F, and the low temperature was 24°F. Then a cold front moved in. The low temperature on January 4 was −5°F.

By how many degrees did the temperature drop from the high on January 3 to the low on January 4?

_____

Write a number model to show how you found your answer.

_____

---

4. The table shows the results of a survey that asked Internet surfers how they most often find sites to visit. Fill in the missing information in the table. Use a protractor to make a circle graph of the results. Do not use the Percent Circle.

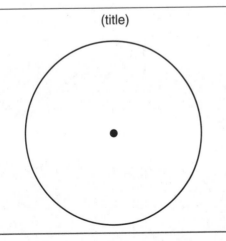

_____
(title)

Method	Number of People	Percent of Total
Word-of-mouth	43	
Printed material	26	
Browsing	14	
Links	9	
Other	8	
Total		

Time to Reflect

The following is an excerpt from the beginning of the poem "Mathematics" by Theoni Pappas. It is taken from *Math Talk: Mathematical Ideas in Poems for Two Voices.* This poem is meant to be read by two people. Each person reads one column, speakers alternating between the two columns.

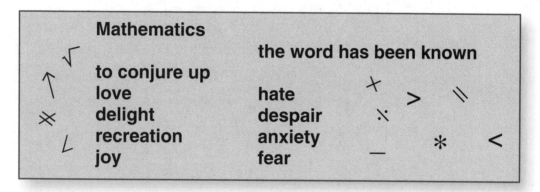

Mathematics

the word has been known

to conjure up
love   hate
delight   despair
recreation anxiety
joy   fear

1. Which words would you use to describe the mathematics in Unit 9? (Think of the poem as a starting point.)

_____

_____

_____

2. Formulas are used in math to solve problems that always require the same information and steps. Think of something you do often that has several steps. Write a formula and explain what it means.

Example $S + W + B + R = T$

   S is the time it takes to squeeze out the toothpaste and put it on the brush.

   W is the time it takes to run the water to get the right temperature.

   B is the time it takes to brush.

   R is the length of time for rinsing my mouth.

   T is the total time needed to brush my teeth.

_____

_____

_____

Math Boxes 9.14

1. Fill in the shape to the right so that it becomes a recognizable figure.

2. Find the ellipse on your Geometry Template. Use it to draw an ellipse below.

3. Write an H inside the regular hexagon. Write a P inside the regular pentagon.

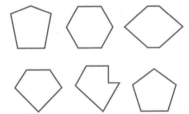

4. Draw the line(s) of symmetry for each figure below.

   a.

   b.

5. Draw an obtuse angle *HIJ*. Measure it.

   Measure of ∠*HIJ* is about _____ °.

Use with Lesson 9.14.

Math Boxes 10.1

1. Translate the word sentences below into number sentences. Do not solve or simplify them.

| < means "is less than" |
| > means "is greater than" |

a. Thirty times one half is equal to fifteen. _____

b. Ten more than the square root of sixty-four is equal to eighteen. _____

c. Nine increased by twelve is less than thirty. _____

d. Twenty-five more than three is greater than ten more than five. _____

e. Sixteen is greater than six more than four. _____

SRB 223

2. Solve.

Solution

a. $n - 54 = -29$ _____

b. $25 * y = 5$ _____

c. $v * 0.01 = 0.54$ _____

d. $376 / w = 94$ _____

e. $12 / b = -4$ _____

SRB 233

3. The formula for the area A of a triangle is

$A = \frac{1}{2} * b * h$

where b is the length of the base and h is the height. Use the formula to calculate the area of the triangle above.

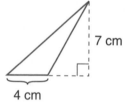

7 cm

4 cm

Area _____

SRB 199

4. Multiply.

a.
```
  5.67
* 20.2
------
```

b.
```
  443.6
* 0.08
------
```

SRB 45 46

5. Multiply or divide. Write your answers in simplest form.

a. $3\frac{8}{9} * 4\frac{5}{6} =$ _____

b. _____ $= \frac{1}{5} * \frac{38}{3}$

c. _____ $= \frac{24}{15} \div \frac{1}{2}$

d. _____ $= \frac{3}{7} * \frac{22}{3}$

e. $\frac{24}{8} \div \frac{12}{7} =$ _____

SRB 86 89 90

Semiregular Tessellations

A **semiregular tessellation** is made up of two or more kinds of regular polygons. In a semiregular tessellation, the arrangement of angles about each **vertex point** looks the same. There are exactly eight different semiregular tessellations. One of the eight is shown below.

Find and draw the other seven semiregular tessellations. The only polygons that are possible in semiregular tessellations are equilateral triangles, squares, regular hexagons, regular octagons, and regular dodecagons. Use your Geometry Template and the template of a regular dodecagon that your teacher will provide.

Experiment first on a separate piece of paper. Then draw the tessellations below and on the next page. Write the name of each tessellation.

1.

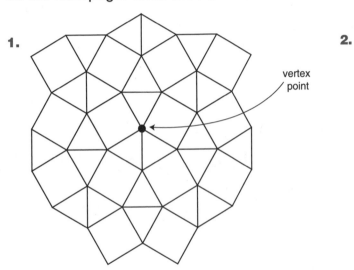

vertex point

Name ___3.3.4.3.4___

2.

Name _____

3.

4.

Name _____

Name _____

Use with Lesson 10.1.

Semiregular Tessellations (cont.)

5.

6.

Name _____

Name _____

7.

8.

Name _____

Name _____

Triangular Numbers

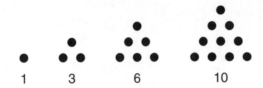

1   3   6   10

Figurate numbers link geometry and arithmetic. They can be shown by dots arranged in geometric patterns. A triangular number is a figurate number that can be shown by a triangular arrangement of dots.

1. Name the first 15 triangular numbers

_____

2. What kind of triangle is used
to display triangular numbers? _____

3. a. Is the *sum* of two triangular numbers always, sometimes, or never another triangular number? Give examples to support your answer.

_____

_____

_____

b. Is the *difference* between two triangular numbers always, sometimes, or never another triangular number? Give examples to support your answer.

_____

_____

_____

c. Is the *product* of two triangular numbers always, sometimes, or never another triangular number? Give examples to support your answer.

_____

_____

_____

My Tessellation

On a separate piece of paper, create an Escher-type translation tessellation using the procedure described on page 326 of your *Student Reference Book.* Experiment with several tessellations until you create one that you especially like.

Trace your final tessellation template in the space below.

In the space below, use your tessellation template to record what your tessellation looks like. Add details to or color your final design.

"Memorable" Numbers

Below is a list of "memorable" numbers. Explain why each number is memorable.
The first one has been done for you.

1. 365   *Number of days in a year*

2. 3.14159… _____

3. 2.54 _____

4. 144 _____

5. 4 _____

6. 52 _____

7. 2,000 _____

8. 1492 _____

9. 90 _____

10. 366 _____

11. 1.6 _____

12. 12 _____

Add two additional numbers to the list of "memorable" numbers, and explain why
they are memorable to you.

13. _____ _____

14. _____ _____

Use with Lesson 10.2.

Math Boxes 10.2

---

1. Find the following measures for a circle with a radius of 3 cm.

Diameter _____ cm

Circumference About _____ cm

Area   About _____ cm²

Explain how you found the area.

_____

_____

_____

195 200

---

2. Evaluate each expression. Use the rules for order of operations. Do not use a calculator.

a. $15 - 3.3 * 4 =$ _____

b. $\frac{20}{4} * 5 + (-8) * 2 =$ _____

c. $7 * 3^2 - \frac{10}{2} =$ _____

d. $8 * (2 + -5) - 4 =$ _____

e. $0.01 + 0.01 * 10 + 0.01 =$ _____

229

---

3. Write each number in scientific notation.

a. A modern personal computer can perform 10,000,000 mathematical operations,

or _____ operations, in one second.

b. A fiber-optic wire carries 1,700,000,000 bits per second, or _____ bits per second.

This is equivalent to 25,000 people,

or _____ people, speaking over a wire roughly the width of a human hair.

c. An ant weighs about 0.00001 kilogram, or _____ kilogram.

d. The approximate weight of the ocean is 1,320,000,000,000,000,000,000 kilograms,

or _____ kilograms.

e. One grass pollen weighs approximately 0.0000000047 gram,

or _____ gram.

Sources: The World Almanac for Kids, 1996; The Sizesaurus

7 8

Rotation Symmetry

Cut out the figures on Activity Sheet 7. Cut along the dashed lines only. Using the procedure demonstrated by your teacher, determine the number of different ways in which each figure can be rotated (but not flipped) so that the image exactly matches the preimage. Record the order of rotation symmetry for each figure.

1.

Order of rotation symmetry _____

2.

Order of rotation symmetry _____

3.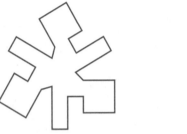

Order of rotation symmetry _____

4.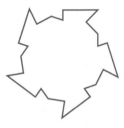

Order of rotation symmetry _____

Challenge

5. The 10 of hearts has point symmetry. When the card is rotated 180°, it looks the same as it did in the original position.

original   180°
position   rotation

The 9 of spades does not have point symmetry. When the card is rotated 180°, it does not look the same as it did in the original position.

original   180°
position   rotation

Which of the cards in an ordinary deck of playing cards (not including face cards) have point symmetry? _____

_____

_____

If you want to learn a magic trick that uses point symmetry with playing cards, see page 321 in your *Student Reference Book*.

Math Boxes 10.3

1. Nancy can read 45 pages an hour. At that rate, about how long will it take her to finish a 380-page book?

_____

SRB
106 239

2. Estimate the answer.

a. $5.25 \div 2.003$ _____

b. $4.29 * 67.1$ _____

c. $80.25 \div 18.93$ _____

d. $52.31 * 19.9$ _____

SRB
45 51

3. Write in number-and-word notation.

a. 68,000 _____

b. 2,500,000 _____

c. 345,000,000 _____

d. 89,000,000,000 _____

e. 7,400,000,000,000 _____

SRB
4

4. Write the following in standard notation.

a. $5.38 * 10^7 =$ _____

b. $6.91 * 10^{-5} =$ _____

c. $3.04 * 10^9 =$ _____

d. _____ $= 9.9011 * 10^5$

e. $7.2 * 10^{-6} =$ _____

SRB
7 8

5. Fill in the blanks in each number sentence.

a. $3 * (90 + 3) = (3 * \underline{\hspace{1cm}}) + (3 * \underline{\hspace{1cm}})$

b. $8 * (40 + 5) = (\underline{\hspace{1cm}} * 40) + (8 * \underline{\hspace{1cm}})$

c. $(10 - 3) * 6 = (10 * \underline{\hspace{1cm}}) - (3 * \underline{\hspace{1cm}})$

d. $(9 * 50) + (9 * \underline{\hspace{1cm}}) = 9 * (\underline{\hspace{1cm}} + 4)$

e. $(7 * 20) - (7 * 3) = \underline{\hspace{1cm}} * (\underline{\hspace{1cm}} - \underline{\hspace{1cm}})$

SRB
230 231

6. Answer each question with an algebraic expression.

a. Tom is $1\frac{1}{2}$ inches taller than he was last year. Last year he was x inches tall. How tall is Tom this year? _____

b. Jane is twice as old as her brother Lyle was 3 years ago. Lyle is y years old now. How old is Jane? _____

SRB
222

Cross Sections of a Clay Cube

Form a clay cube. Draw your prediction of the shape of the cross section that will be formed by the first cut shown below. After making the cut, draw the actual shape and describe (name) the shape. Re-form the cube and repeat these steps for the other cuts.

Clay Cube	Predicted Shape of Cross Section	Actual Shape of Cross Section	Description of Shape

Use with Lesson 10.4.

Cross Sections of a Clay Cylinder

Form a clay cylinder. Draw your prediction of the shape of the cross section that will be formed by the first cut shown below. After making the cut, draw the actual shape and describe (name) the shape. Re-form the cylinder and repeat these steps for the other cuts.

Clay Cylinder	Predicted Shape of Cross Section	Actual Shape of Cross Section	Description of Shape

Date _____ Time _____

Cross Sections of a Clay Cone

Form a clay cone. Draw your prediction of the shape of the cross section that will be formed by the first cut shown below. After making the cut, draw the actual shape and describe (name) the shape. Re-form the cone and repeat these steps for the other cuts.

Clay Cone	Predicted Shape of Cross Section	Actual Shape of Cross Section	Description of Shape

398

Use with Lesson 10.4.

Math Boxes 10.4

---

1. Translate the word sentences below into number sentences. Do not solve or simplify them.

| < means "is less than" |
| > means "is greater than" |

a. Five and one half is less than six.

_____

b. Eighteen more than twelve is greater than two times seven.

_____

c. One tenth times forty is equal to four.

_____

d. Three more than fourteen divided by seven is equal to five.

_____

e. Nine decreased by four is less than seventeen decreased by two.

_____

---

2. Solve.

Solution

a. $15 * x = 60$ _____

b. $\frac{q}{10} = 150$ _____

c. $m + (-28) = -5$ _____

d. $\frac{36}{s} + 5 = 9$ _____

e. $-1 * t = -15$ _____

---

3. The formula for finding the volume of a rectangular prism is

$V = l * w * h$

where *l* is the length of the prism, *w* is the width, and *h* is the height. Use the formula to calculate the volume of this rectangular prism.

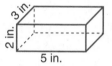

Volume _____

---

4. Multiply.

a.   6.76
     * 0.005

b.   14.09
     * 2.25

---

5. Multiply or divide. Write your answers in simplest form.

a. $1\frac{3}{7} * 2\frac{1}{5} =$ _____

b. $3\frac{6}{8} * \frac{28}{6} =$ _____

c. $5\frac{1}{10} \div 2\frac{5}{4} =$ _____

d. $\frac{46}{3} \div 20 =$ _____

e. $5\frac{3}{5} * \frac{1}{8} =$ _____

Venn Diagram

In what ways are a doughnut and a coffee mug similar? In what ways are they different? Record your thoughts in the Venn diagram below.

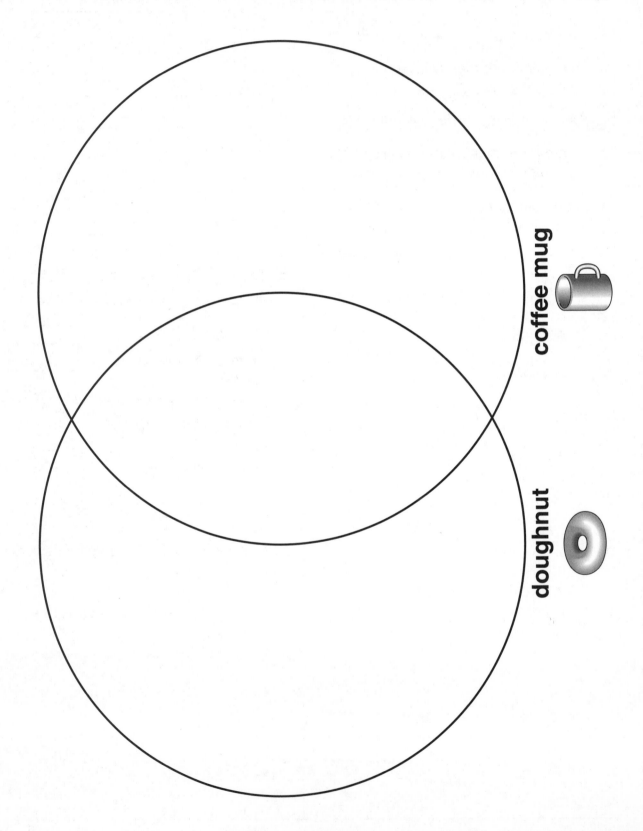

Use with Lesson 10.5.

Math Boxes 10.5

1. Find the following measures for a circle with a radius of 4 cm.

Diameter _____ cm

Circumference   About _____ cm

Area   About _____ cm^2

Explain how you found the circumference.

_____

_____

_____

2. Evaluate each expression. Use the rules for order of operations. Do not use a calculator.

a. $4 * \frac{7}{2} + 7 =$ _____

b. $8 + (-15) * 6 =$ _____

c. $\frac{6^2}{9} + 3 * 4 =$ _____

d. $8 + 7 - (-2) * 5 =$ _____

e. $12 / 6 + 9 * 3 =$ _____

3. Write each number in scientific notation.

a. There are about 12,000,000,000 chickens in the world,

or _____ chickens.

b. A trained tracking dog can follow the sweat scent left by a foot when only

0.00000000004 gram of sweat, or _____ gram, is present.

c. There are 60,000,000,000,000 cells, or _____ cells, in the body.

d. When a toilet is flushed, between 5,000,000,000 and 10,000,000,000 water droplets,

or between _____ and _____ water droplets,
are released into the air.

e. The smallest dust particles are about 0.01 centimeter, or _____ centimeter,
in width.

Sources: The Top Ten of Everything, 1996; The Sizesaurus

Rubber-Sheet Geometry

You and your partner will need the following materials: 3 latex gloves, a straightedge, a pair of scissors, and a permanent marker.

Step 1 Cut the fingers and thumb off of each glove.

Step 2 Make a vertical cut through each of the three "cylinders" that remain. The cutting creates three rubber sheets.

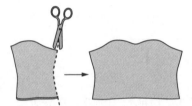

Step 3 Use a permanent marker and a straightedge to draw the following figures on the rubber sheets. Draw the figures large enough to fill most of the sheet.

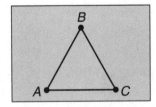
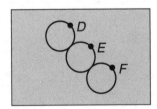
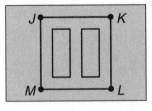

Step 4 Work with your partner to stretch the rubber sheets to see what other figures you can make.

Step 5 Complete journal page 403.

Rubber-Sheet Geometry (cont.)

1. Experiment with the figures on your rubber sheets. Circle any of the figures in the right-hand column that are topologically equivalent to the corresponding original figure in the left-hand column.

Original Figure	Transformed Figures
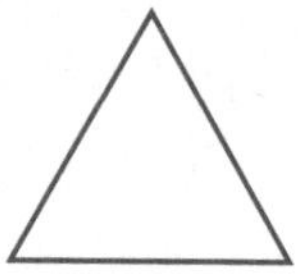	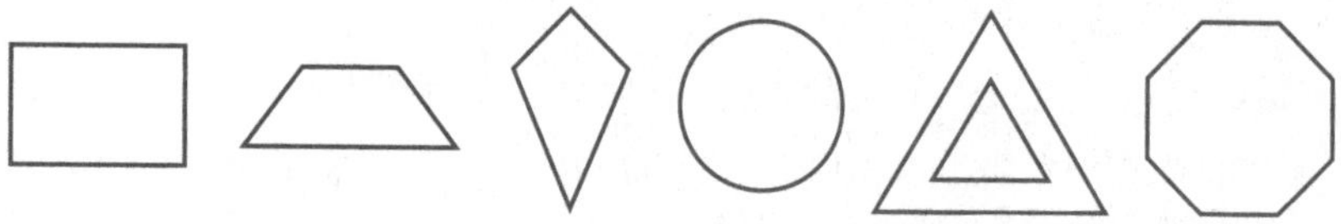
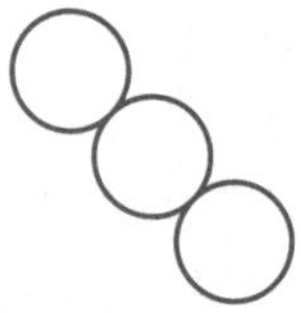	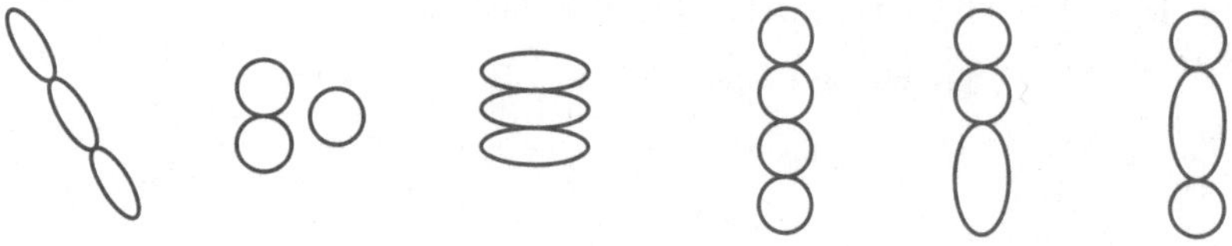
	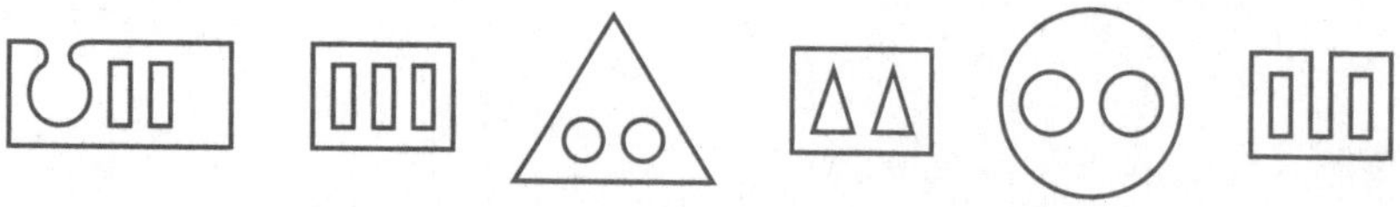

2. Choose one of the above figures that you did not circle and explain why it is not topologically equivalent to its original figure.

_____

_____

_____

Constructing a Möbius Strip

Follow the steps below to make a Möbius strip.

Materials

- ❑ a sheet of newspaper or adding machine tape
- ❑ scissors
- ❑ tape
- ❑ a bright color crayon, marker, or pencil

Step 1 Cut a strip of newspaper about $1\frac{1}{2}$ inches wide and as long as possible, or cut a strip of adding machine tape about 2 feet long.

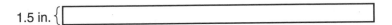

1.5 in.

Step 2 Put the ends of the strip together as though you were making a simple loop.

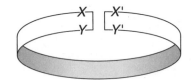

Step 3 Give one end of the strip a half-twist and tape the two ends together.

You have just made what mathematicians call a **Möbius strip.** How is it different from a simple loop of paper? Do you notice anything special about it?

_____

_____

_____

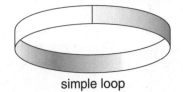

simple loop

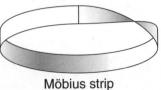

Möbius strip

Math Boxes 10.6

---

1. Grant collects marbles. His favorite store sells marbles for 69 cents per marble. How many marbles can he buy if he has $15.00?

_____

2. Estimate the answer.

  a. $44.2 * 37$ _____

  b. $708 \div 0.52$ _____

  c. $625.7 \div 8.3$ _____

  d. $99.4 * 3.7$ _____

---

3. Write each number in number-and-word notation.

  a. 52,000 _____

  b. 6,500,000 _____

  c. 945,000,000 _____

  d. 77,000,000,000 _____

  e. 12,500,000,000,000 _____

4. Write the following in standard notation.

  a. $2.73 * 10^5 =$ _____

  b. $1.03 * 10^{-4} =$ _____

  c. _____ $= 4.226 * 10^8$

  d. _____ $= 8.001 * 10^{-2}$

  e. $5.435 * 10^9 =$ _____

---

5. Fill in the blanks in each number sentence.

  a. $8 * (30 + 4) = (8 * \underline{\hspace{1cm}}) + (8 * \underline{\hspace{1cm}})$

  b. $9 * (20 + 7) = (\underline{\hspace{1cm}} * 20) + (9 * \underline{\hspace{1cm}})$

  c. $(50 - 3) * 6 = (50 * \underline{\hspace{1cm}}) - (3 * \underline{\hspace{1cm}})$

  d. $(8 * 70) + (8 * \underline{\hspace{1cm}}) = 8 * (\underline{\hspace{1cm}} + 7)$

  e. $(6 * 50) - (6 * 9) = \underline{\hspace{1cm}} * (\underline{\hspace{1cm}} - \underline{\hspace{1cm}})$

---

6. Answer each question with an algebraic expression.

  a. Rudolph now has three times as many customers for baby-sitting as he had one year ago. Then he had x customers. How many customers does he have now?

_____

  b. Alicia earns $2.00 each time she helps mow the lawn. In June, she helped y times. In July, she helped 2 more times than in June. How much did she earn in July?

_____

Experimenting with Möbius Strips

1. How many sides do you
   think your Möbius strip has? _____ sides

2. Use a marker to shade one side of your Möbius strip.

3. Now how many sides do you think your Möbius strip has? Explain.

   _____

4. How many edges do you
   think your Möbius strip has? _____ edges

5. Use your marker to color one edge of your Möbius strip.

6. Now how many edges do you think your Möbius strip has? Explain.

   _____

   _____

Cutting Möbius strips also leads to some surprising results.

7. Predict what will happen if you cut your Möbius strip in half lengthwise.

   _____

   _____

8. Now cut your Möbius strip in half lengthwise. How many strips did you get? _____ strips

   Compare the lengths and widths of the new strip and the original strip.

   Describe your observations. _____

   _____

How many half-twists
does your new strip have? _____ half-twists

9. Make another Möbius strip and cut it one-third of the way from the
   edge. You may find it helpful to draw lines on the strip before cutting.

   What happened? _____

   _____

   _____

Experimenting with Möbius Strips (cont.)

10. Make another Möbius strip and a simple loop. Then tape the loop and the Möbius strip together at right angles.

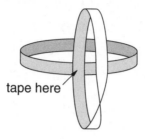

tape here

Cut both the Möbius strip and the loop in half lengthwise. What happened?

_____

_____

_____

_____

11. Experiment with cutting Möbius strips both in half and in thirds lengthwise. Try putting two or more half-twists in the band before you tape it. Describe what you did as well as your results.

_____

_____

_____

_____

Imagine a bottle with no inside. Felix Klein was a German mathematician in the late 1800s. He designed a bottle with no inside. If you poured water into the bottle, it would flow right back out. Interestingly, if you cut the Klein bottle in half, you get two Möbius strips. (Actually, a real Klein bottle cannot be constructed, since the neck of the bottle can't pass back through without making a hole.)

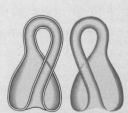

Reviewing Unit 10 Geometry Topics

1. Circle the polygons that you can tessellate.

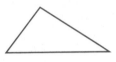

2. Use your Geometry Template to draw the result of each rotation. Point *R* is the point of rotation.

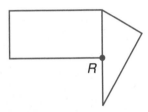

original figure   90° clockwise   180° counterclockwise   270° clockwise

Predict the shape of each cross section. Draw your prediction to the right of the illustration.

3.    **4.**

5. Put an X through the figure that is not topologically equivalent to the original figure.

Original
figure

                                              Use with Lesson 10.6.

Time to Reflect

1. Which activity in this unit did you like best?

_____

_____

_____

_____

_____

2. Did any of the activities make you curious about further mathematical study? Which one? What questions would you like to have answered about it?

_____

_____

_____

_____

_____

3. Think about any art (figurines, posters, drawings, calendar photos) that you have in your room (or anywhere in your home). Do any of them use any kind of symmetry that you have studied this year? Describe the art and the kind of symmetry it has. If you don't have anything in your home, look around the classroom to find something to describe.

_____

_____

_____

_____

_____

Reference

Metric System

Units of Length
1 kilometer (km)	= 1000 meters (m)
1 meter	= 10 decimeters (dm)
	= 100 centimeters (cm)
	= 1000 millimeters (mm)
1 decimeter	= 10 centimeters
1 centimeter	= 10 millimeters

Units of Area
1 square meter (m^2)	= 100 square decimeters (dm^2)
	= 10,000 square centimeters (cm^2)
1 square decimeter	= 100 square centimeters
1 are (a)	= 100 square meters
1 hectare (ha)	= 100 ares
1 square kilometer (km^2)	= 100 hectares

Units of Volume
1 cubic meter (m^3)	= 1000 cubic decimeters (dm^3)
	= 1,000,000 cubic centimeters (cm^3)
1 cubic decimeter	= 1000 cubic centimeters

Units of Capacity
1 kiloliter (kL)	= 1000 liters (L)
1 liter	= 1000 milliliters (mL)

Units of Mass
1 metric ton (t)	= 1000 kilograms (kg)
1 kilogram	= 1000 grams (g)
1 gram	= 1000 milligrams (mg)

Units of Time
1 century	= 100 years
1 decade	= 10 years
1 year (yr)	= 12 months
	= 52 weeks (plus one or two days)
	= 365 days (366 days in a leap year)
1 month (mo)	= 28, 29, 30, or 31 days
1 week (wk)	= 7 days
1 day (d)	= 24 hours
1 hour (hr)	= 60 minutes
1 minute (min)	= 60 seconds (sec)

U.S. Customary System

Units of Length
1 mile (mi)	= 1760 yards (yd)
	= 5280 feet (ft)
1 yard	= 3 feet
	= 36 inches (in.)
1 foot	= 12 inches

Units of Area
1 square yard (yd^2)	= 9 square feet (ft^2)
	= 1296 square inches ($in.^2$)
1 square foot	= 144 square inches
1 acre	= 43,560 square feet
1 square mile (mi^2)	= 640 acres

Units of Volume
1 cubic yard (yd^3)	= 27 cubic feet (ft^3)
1 cubic foot	= 1728 cubic inches ($in.^3$)

Units of Capacity
1 gallon (gal)	= 4 quarts (qt)
1 quart	= 2 pints (pt)
1 pint	= 2 cups (c)
1 cup	= 8 fluid ounces (fl oz)
1 fluid ounce	= 2 tablespoons (tbs)
1 tablespoon	= 3 teaspoons (tsp)

Units of Weight
1 ton (T)	= 2000 pounds (lb)
1 pound	= 16 ounces (oz)

System Equivalents
1 inch is about 2.5 cm (2.54)
1 kilometer is about 0.6 mile (0.621)
1 mile is about 1.6 kilometers (1.609)
1 meter is about 39 inches (39.37)
1 liter is about 1.1 quarts (1.057)
1 ounce is about 28 grams (28.350)
1 kilogram is about 2.2 pounds (2.205)
1 hectare is about 2.5 acres (2.47)

Rules for Order of Operations

1. Do operations within parentheses or other grouping symbols before doing anything else.
2. Calculate all powers.
3. Do multiplications or divisions in order, from left to right.
4. Then do additions or subtractions in order, from left to right.

Reference

Symbols

+	plus or positive
−	minus or negative
$*$, $\times$	multiplied by
$\div$, /	divided by
=	is equal to
≠	is not equal to
<	is less than
>	is greater than
≤	is less than or equal to
≥	is greater than or equal to
x^n	nth power of x
$\sqrt{x}$	square root of x
%	percent
$\frac{a}{b}$, $a{:}b$, a/b	ratio of a to b or a divided by b or the fraction $\frac{a}{b}$
°	degree
(a,b)	ordered pair
$\overleftrightarrow{AS}$	line AS
$\overline{AS}$	line segment AS
$\overrightarrow{AS}$	ray AS
∟	right angle
⊥	is perpendicular to
∥	is parallel to
△ABC	triangle ABC
∠ABC	angle ABC
∠B	angle B

Place-Value Chart

trillions	100B	10B	billions	100M	10M	millions	hundred-thousands	ten-thousands	thousands	hundreds	tens	ones	.	tenths	hundredths	thousandths
1000 billions			1000 millions			1,000,000s	100,000s	10,000s	1000s	100s	10s	1s	.	0.1s	0.01s	0.001s
10^{12}	10^{11}	10^{10}	10^9	10^8	10^7	10^6	10^5	10^4	10^3	10^2	10^1	10^0	.	10^{-1}	10^{-2}	10^{-3}

Probability Meter

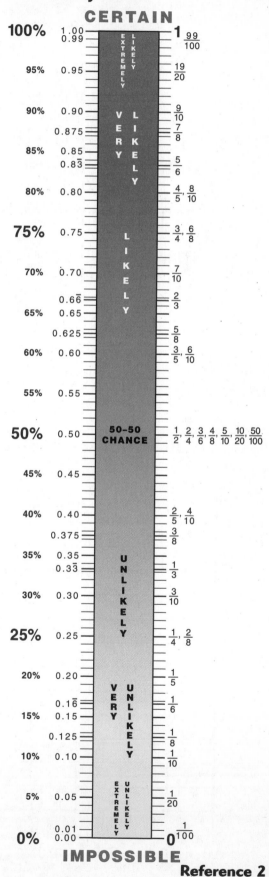

Reference

Latitude and Longitude

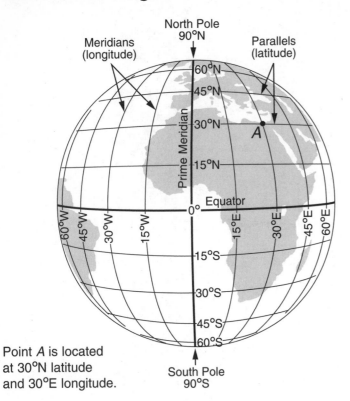

Point *A* is located at 30°N latitude and 30°E longitude.

Rational Numbers

Rule	Example
$\dfrac{a}{b} = \dfrac{n*a}{n*b}$	$\dfrac{2}{3} = \dfrac{4*2}{4*3} = \dfrac{8}{12}$
$\dfrac{a}{b} = \dfrac{a/n}{b/n}$	$\dfrac{8}{12} = \dfrac{8/4}{12/4} = \dfrac{2}{3}$
$\dfrac{a}{a} = a * \dfrac{1}{a} = 1$	$\dfrac{4}{4} = 4 * \dfrac{1}{4} = 1$
$\dfrac{a}{b} + \dfrac{c}{b} = \dfrac{a+c}{b}$	$\dfrac{3}{5} + \dfrac{1}{5} = \dfrac{3+1}{5} = \dfrac{4}{5}$
$\dfrac{a}{b} - \dfrac{c}{b} = \dfrac{a-c}{b}$	$\dfrac{3}{5} - \dfrac{1}{5} = \dfrac{3-1}{5} = \dfrac{2}{5}$
$\dfrac{a}{b} * \dfrac{c}{d} = \dfrac{a*c}{b*d}$	$\dfrac{1}{4} * \dfrac{2}{3} = \dfrac{1*2}{4*3} = \dfrac{2}{12}$

To compare, add, or subtract fractions:

1. Find a common denominator.

2. Rewrite fractions as equivalent fractions with the common denominator.

3. Compare, add, or subtract these fractions.

Fraction-Stick and Decimal Number-Line Chart

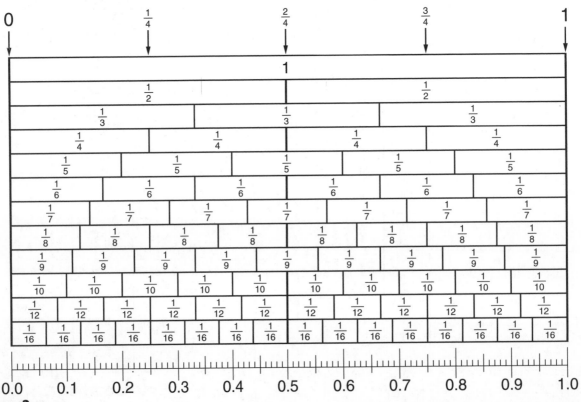

Reference

Equivalent Fractions, Decimals, and Percents

															Decimal	Percent
$\frac{1}{2}$	$\frac{2}{4}$	$\frac{3}{6}$	$\frac{4}{8}$	$\frac{5}{10}$	$\frac{6}{12}$	$\frac{7}{14}$	$\frac{8}{16}$	$\frac{9}{18}$	$\frac{10}{20}$	$\frac{11}{22}$	$\frac{12}{24}$	$\frac{13}{26}$	$\frac{14}{28}$	$\frac{15}{30}$	0.5	50%
$\frac{1}{3}$	$\frac{2}{6}$	$\frac{3}{9}$	$\frac{4}{12}$	$\frac{5}{15}$	$\frac{6}{18}$	$\frac{7}{21}$	$\frac{8}{24}$	$\frac{9}{27}$	$\frac{10}{30}$	$\frac{11}{33}$	$\frac{12}{36}$	$\frac{13}{39}$	$\frac{14}{42}$	$\frac{15}{45}$	$0.\overline{3}$	$33\frac{1}{3}\%$
$\frac{2}{3}$	$\frac{4}{6}$	$\frac{6}{9}$	$\frac{8}{12}$	$\frac{10}{15}$	$\frac{12}{18}$	$\frac{14}{21}$	$\frac{16}{24}$	$\frac{18}{27}$	$\frac{20}{30}$	$\frac{22}{33}$	$\frac{24}{36}$	$\frac{26}{39}$	$\frac{28}{42}$	$\frac{30}{45}$	$0.\overline{6}$	$66\frac{2}{3}\%$
$\frac{1}{4}$	$\frac{2}{8}$	$\frac{3}{12}$	$\frac{4}{16}$	$\frac{5}{20}$	$\frac{6}{24}$	$\frac{7}{28}$	$\frac{8}{32}$	$\frac{9}{36}$	$\frac{10}{40}$	$\frac{11}{44}$	$\frac{12}{48}$	$\frac{13}{52}$	$\frac{14}{56}$	$\frac{15}{60}$	0.25	25%
$\frac{3}{4}$	$\frac{6}{8}$	$\frac{9}{12}$	$\frac{12}{16}$	$\frac{15}{20}$	$\frac{18}{24}$	$\frac{21}{28}$	$\frac{24}{32}$	$\frac{27}{36}$	$\frac{30}{40}$	$\frac{33}{44}$	$\frac{36}{48}$	$\frac{39}{52}$	$\frac{42}{56}$	$\frac{45}{60}$	0.75	75%
$\frac{1}{5}$	$\frac{2}{10}$	$\frac{3}{15}$	$\frac{4}{20}$	$\frac{5}{25}$	$\frac{6}{30}$	$\frac{7}{35}$	$\frac{8}{40}$	$\frac{9}{45}$	$\frac{10}{50}$	$\frac{11}{55}$	$\frac{12}{60}$	$\frac{13}{65}$	$\frac{14}{70}$	$\frac{15}{75}$	0.2	20%
$\frac{2}{5}$	$\frac{4}{10}$	$\frac{6}{15}$	$\frac{8}{20}$	$\frac{10}{25}$	$\frac{12}{30}$	$\frac{14}{35}$	$\frac{16}{40}$	$\frac{18}{45}$	$\frac{20}{50}$	$\frac{22}{55}$	$\frac{24}{60}$	$\frac{26}{65}$	$\frac{28}{70}$	$\frac{30}{75}$	0.4	40%
$\frac{3}{5}$	$\frac{6}{10}$	$\frac{9}{15}$	$\frac{12}{20}$	$\frac{15}{25}$	$\frac{18}{30}$	$\frac{21}{35}$	$\frac{24}{40}$	$\frac{27}{45}$	$\frac{30}{50}$	$\frac{33}{55}$	$\frac{36}{60}$	$\frac{39}{65}$	$\frac{42}{70}$	$\frac{45}{75}$	0.6	60%
$\frac{4}{5}$	$\frac{8}{10}$	$\frac{12}{15}$	$\frac{16}{20}$	$\frac{20}{25}$	$\frac{24}{30}$	$\frac{28}{35}$	$\frac{32}{40}$	$\frac{36}{45}$	$\frac{40}{50}$	$\frac{44}{55}$	$\frac{48}{60}$	$\frac{52}{65}$	$\frac{56}{70}$	$\frac{60}{75}$	0.8	80%
$\frac{1}{6}$	$\frac{2}{12}$	$\frac{3}{18}$	$\frac{4}{24}$	$\frac{5}{30}$	$\frac{6}{36}$	$\frac{7}{42}$	$\frac{8}{48}$	$\frac{9}{54}$	$\frac{10}{60}$	$\frac{11}{66}$	$\frac{12}{72}$	$\frac{13}{78}$	$\frac{14}{84}$	$\frac{15}{90}$	$0.1\overline{6}$	$16\frac{2}{3}\%$
$\frac{5}{6}$	$\frac{10}{12}$	$\frac{15}{18}$	$\frac{20}{24}$	$\frac{25}{30}$	$\frac{30}{36}$	$\frac{35}{42}$	$\frac{40}{48}$	$\frac{45}{54}$	$\frac{50}{60}$	$\frac{55}{66}$	$\frac{60}{72}$	$\frac{65}{78}$	$\frac{70}{84}$	$\frac{75}{90}$	$0.8\overline{3}$	$83\frac{1}{3}\%$
$\frac{1}{7}$	$\frac{2}{14}$	$\frac{3}{21}$	$\frac{4}{28}$	$\frac{5}{35}$	$\frac{6}{42}$	$\frac{7}{49}$	$\frac{8}{56}$	$\frac{9}{63}$	$\frac{10}{70}$	$\frac{11}{77}$	$\frac{12}{84}$	$\frac{13}{91}$	$\frac{14}{98}$	$\frac{15}{105}$	0.143	14.3%
$\frac{2}{7}$	$\frac{4}{14}$	$\frac{6}{21}$	$\frac{8}{28}$	$\frac{10}{35}$	$\frac{12}{42}$	$\frac{14}{49}$	$\frac{16}{56}$	$\frac{18}{63}$	$\frac{20}{70}$	$\frac{22}{77}$	$\frac{24}{84}$	$\frac{26}{91}$	$\frac{28}{98}$	$\frac{30}{105}$	0.286	28.6%
$\frac{3}{7}$	$\frac{6}{14}$	$\frac{9}{21}$	$\frac{12}{28}$	$\frac{15}{35}$	$\frac{18}{42}$	$\frac{21}{49}$	$\frac{24}{56}$	$\frac{27}{63}$	$\frac{30}{70}$	$\frac{33}{77}$	$\frac{36}{84}$	$\frac{39}{91}$	$\frac{42}{98}$	$\frac{45}{105}$	0.429	42.9%
$\frac{4}{7}$	$\frac{8}{14}$	$\frac{12}{21}$	$\frac{16}{28}$	$\frac{20}{35}$	$\frac{24}{42}$	$\frac{28}{49}$	$\frac{32}{56}$	$\frac{36}{63}$	$\frac{40}{70}$	$\frac{44}{77}$	$\frac{48}{84}$	$\frac{52}{91}$	$\frac{56}{98}$	$\frac{60}{105}$	0.571	57.1%
$\frac{5}{7}$	$\frac{10}{14}$	$\frac{15}{21}$	$\frac{20}{28}$	$\frac{25}{35}$	$\frac{30}{42}$	$\frac{35}{49}$	$\frac{40}{56}$	$\frac{45}{63}$	$\frac{50}{70}$	$\frac{55}{77}$	$\frac{60}{84}$	$\frac{65}{91}$	$\frac{70}{98}$	$\frac{75}{105}$	0.714	71.4%
$\frac{6}{7}$	$\frac{12}{14}$	$\frac{18}{21}$	$\frac{24}{28}$	$\frac{30}{35}$	$\frac{36}{42}$	$\frac{42}{49}$	$\frac{48}{56}$	$\frac{54}{63}$	$\frac{60}{70}$	$\frac{66}{77}$	$\frac{72}{84}$	$\frac{78}{91}$	$\frac{84}{98}$	$\frac{90}{105}$	0.857	85.7%
$\frac{1}{8}$	$\frac{2}{16}$	$\frac{3}{24}$	$\frac{4}{32}$	$\frac{5}{40}$	$\frac{6}{48}$	$\frac{7}{56}$	$\frac{8}{64}$	$\frac{9}{72}$	$\frac{10}{80}$	$\frac{11}{88}$	$\frac{12}{96}$	$\frac{13}{104}$	$\frac{14}{112}$	$\frac{15}{120}$	0.125	$12\frac{1}{2}\%$
$\frac{3}{8}$	$\frac{6}{16}$	$\frac{9}{24}$	$\frac{12}{32}$	$\frac{15}{40}$	$\frac{18}{48}$	$\frac{21}{56}$	$\frac{24}{64}$	$\frac{27}{72}$	$\frac{30}{80}$	$\frac{33}{88}$	$\frac{36}{96}$	$\frac{39}{104}$	$\frac{42}{112}$	$\frac{45}{120}$	0.375	$37\frac{1}{2}\%$
$\frac{5}{8}$	$\frac{10}{16}$	$\frac{15}{24}$	$\frac{20}{32}$	$\frac{25}{40}$	$\frac{30}{48}$	$\frac{35}{56}$	$\frac{40}{64}$	$\frac{45}{72}$	$\frac{50}{80}$	$\frac{55}{88}$	$\frac{60}{96}$	$\frac{65}{104}$	$\frac{70}{112}$	$\frac{75}{120}$	0.625	$62\frac{1}{2}\%$
$\frac{7}{8}$	$\frac{14}{16}$	$\frac{21}{24}$	$\frac{28}{32}$	$\frac{35}{40}$	$\frac{42}{48}$	$\frac{49}{56}$	$\frac{56}{64}$	$\frac{63}{72}$	$\frac{70}{80}$	$\frac{77}{88}$	$\frac{84}{96}$	$\frac{91}{104}$	$\frac{98}{112}$	$\frac{105}{120}$	0.875	$87\frac{1}{2}\%$
$\frac{1}{9}$	$\frac{2}{18}$	$\frac{3}{27}$	$\frac{4}{36}$	$\frac{5}{45}$	$\frac{6}{54}$	$\frac{7}{63}$	$\frac{8}{72}$	$\frac{9}{81}$	$\frac{10}{90}$	$\frac{11}{99}$	$\frac{12}{108}$	$\frac{13}{117}$	$\frac{14}{126}$	$\frac{15}{135}$	$0.\overline{1}$	$11\frac{1}{9}\%$
$\frac{2}{9}$	$\frac{4}{18}$	$\frac{6}{27}$	$\frac{8}{36}$	$\frac{10}{45}$	$\frac{12}{54}$	$\frac{14}{63}$	$\frac{16}{72}$	$\frac{18}{81}$	$\frac{20}{90}$	$\frac{22}{99}$	$\frac{24}{108}$	$\frac{26}{117}$	$\frac{28}{126}$	$\frac{30}{135}$	$0.\overline{2}$	$22\frac{2}{9}\%$
$\frac{4}{9}$	$\frac{8}{18}$	$\frac{12}{27}$	$\frac{16}{36}$	$\frac{20}{45}$	$\frac{24}{54}$	$\frac{28}{63}$	$\frac{32}{72}$	$\frac{36}{81}$	$\frac{40}{90}$	$\frac{44}{99}$	$\frac{48}{108}$	$\frac{52}{117}$	$\frac{56}{126}$	$\frac{60}{135}$	$0.\overline{4}$	$44\frac{4}{9}\%$
$\frac{5}{9}$	$\frac{10}{18}$	$\frac{15}{27}$	$\frac{20}{36}$	$\frac{25}{45}$	$\frac{30}{54}$	$\frac{35}{63}$	$\frac{40}{72}$	$\frac{45}{81}$	$\frac{50}{90}$	$\frac{55}{99}$	$\frac{60}{108}$	$\frac{65}{117}$	$\frac{70}{126}$	$\frac{75}{135}$	$0.\overline{5}$	$55\frac{5}{9}\%$
$\frac{7}{9}$	$\frac{14}{18}$	$\frac{21}{27}$	$\frac{28}{36}$	$\frac{35}{45}$	$\frac{42}{54}$	$\frac{49}{63}$	$\frac{56}{72}$	$\frac{63}{81}$	$\frac{70}{90}$	$\frac{77}{99}$	$\frac{84}{108}$	$\frac{91}{117}$	$\frac{98}{126}$	$\frac{105}{135}$	$0.\overline{7}$	$77\frac{7}{9}\%$
$\frac{8}{9}$	$\frac{16}{18}$	$\frac{24}{27}$	$\frac{32}{36}$	$\frac{40}{45}$	$\frac{48}{54}$	$\frac{56}{63}$	$\frac{64}{72}$	$\frac{72}{81}$	$\frac{80}{90}$	$\frac{88}{99}$	$\frac{96}{108}$	$\frac{104}{117}$	$\frac{112}{126}$	$\frac{120}{135}$	$0.\overline{8}$	$88\frac{8}{9}\%$

Note: The decimals for sevenths have been rounded to the nearest thousandth.

Algebra Election Cards, Set 1

Find:

x squared

x to the fourth power

$1/x$

Insert parentheses in

$10 * x - 10$

so that its value is greater than 0 and less than 100.

$$T = B - (2 * \tfrac{H}{1000})$$

If $B = 80$ and $H = 100x$, what does T equal?

Tell whether each is true or false.

$10 * x > 100$

$\tfrac{1}{2} * x * 100 < 10^3$

$x^3 * 1000 > 4 * 10^4$

Find n. (*Hint: n* could be a negative number.)

$1000 + n = x$

$1000 + n = -x$

Find n. (*Hint: n* could be a negative number.)

$n + 10 = x$

$n - 10 = x$

Find n.

$n = (2 * x) / 10$

$n + 1 = (2 * x)$

Which number is this?

$x * 10^2$?

$x * 10^5$?

Complete.

$x * 10^6 =$ ____ million

$x * 10^9 =$ ____ billion

$x * 10^{12} =$ ____

What is the value of *n*?

$$n = ((5 * x) - 4) / 2$$

Suppose you earn x dollars per hour. Complete the table.

Time	Earnings
1 hr	$
2 hr	$
4 hr	$
10 hr	$

A boulder dropped off a cliff falls approximately $16 * x^2$ feet in x seconds.

How many feet is that?

What is the value of *n*?

$-20 + x = n$

$-100 + (-x) = n$

What is the value of *n*?

$20 + (-x) = n$

$-20 - (-x) = n$

Which is greater:

x^2 or 10^3?

x^3 or 10^4?

Which is less:

$\tfrac{x^3}{10}$ or $(x + 10)^2$?

$10 * x^2$ or $(x + 10)^3$?

Algebra Election Cards, Set 2

What is n?

$$5 + 2 * x = n + x$$

$x + \triangle$ 200 oz

1 $\triangle$ weighs ____ ounces.

Insert parentheses so that the equation is true.

$$10 * x + 4 = 10 * x + 40$$

Is point (x, x) above, below, or on the line through points A and B?

A (0, 30)   B (60, 30)

Tell which is correct for each: <, =, or >.

$x < = > 30 - x$

$x < = > 20 - x$

$x < = > 10 - x$

Name a number n such that $x - n$ is a negative number greater than -10.

Suppose you have 10 $\boxed{+}$ markers and $2 * x$ $\boxed{-}$ markers.

What is your balance?

Suppose you have x $\boxed{+}$ markers and 40 $\boxed{-}$ markers.

What is your balance?

Is point (x, x) to the left of, to the right of, or on the line through points A and B?

B (30, 60)   A (30, 0)

What is the value of n?

$$10 + (-x) = n$$

$$-10 - (-x) = n$$

What is the median of 4, 8, 12, 13, and x?

If $(2 * x) + n = 100$, what is the value of n?

Is $1/x$ greater than, less than, or equal to $\frac{1}{10}$?

Subtract.

$$x - 100 = ?$$

$$x - (-100) = ?$$

Add.

$$-25 + x = ?$$

$$x + 3 - 10 = ?$$

Suppose you travel x miles per hour. Complete the table.

Time	Distance
1 hr	
2 hr	
4 hr	
10 hr	

Rotation Symmetry

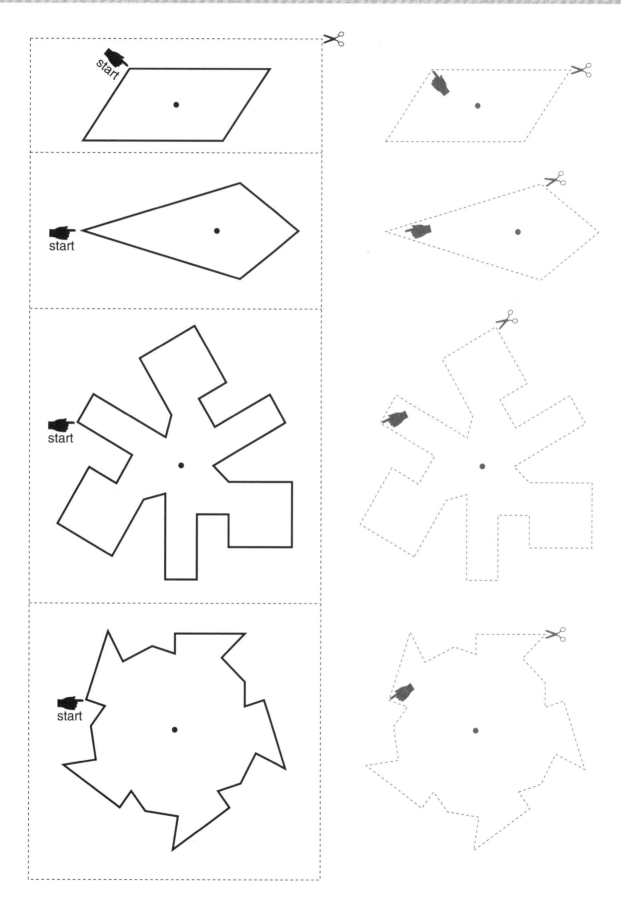